How to
INTEGRATE *the*
CURRICULA
Third Edition

The poet, who navigates the stars . . .
The writer, who touches the soul . . .
The inventor, who notes nature's ways . . .
The friend, who connects one with another . . .

How to _____
INTEGRATE *the*
CURRICULA
Third Edition

___*Robin Fogarty*

Foreword by **Heidi Hayes Jacobs**

CORWIN
A SAGE Company

Copyright © 2009 by Corwin

For information:

Corwin
A SAGE Company
2455 Teller Road
Thousand Oaks, California 91320
(800) 233-9936
Fax: (800) 417-2466
www.corwinpress.com

SAGE India Pvt. Ltd.
B 1/I 1 Mohan Cooperative Industrial Area
Mathura Road, New Delhi
India 110 044

SAGE Ltd.
1 Oliver's Yard
55 City Road
London EC1Y 1SP
United Kingdom

SAGE Asia-Pacific Pte. Ltd.
33 Pekin Street #02-01
Far East Square
Singapore 048763

Printed in the United States of America.

Library of Congress Cataloging-in-Publication Data

Fogarty, Robin.
How to integrate the curricula / Robin Fogarty.—3rd ed.
    p. cm.
Includes bibliographical references and index.
ISBN 978-1-4129-3888-4 (cloth : alk. paper)
ISBN 978-1-4129-3889-1 (pbk. : alk. paper)

    1. Education—Curricula—United States—Handbooks, manuals, etc. 2. Interdisciplinary approach in education—United States—Handbooks, manuals, etc. I. Title.

LB1570.F655 2009
375—dc22   2008056034

This book is printed on acid-free paper.

09   10   11   12   13   10   9   8   7   6   5   4   3   2   1

Acquisitions Editor:	Hudson Perigo
Editorial Assistant:	Lesley K. Blake
Production Editor:	Cassandra Margaret Seibel
Copy Editor:	Sarah J. Duffy
Typesetter:	C&M Digitals (P) Ltd.
Proofreader:	Carole Quandt
Indexer:	Jean Casalegno
Cover Designer:	Anthony Paular
Graphic Designer:	Scott Van Atta

Contents

Foreword

In the spirit of continuous learning, Dr. Robin Fogarty has added new insight into this third edition of *How to Integrate the Curricula.* Her initial contribution to the field of education was to give teachers clear and practical images and exercises that provoked new perspectives on curriculum making. In this edition, she builds and adds useful suggestions that deepen the work. She has added refined practices, engaging strategies, and targeted research references to support her models for curriculum design.

Ultimately, this is a practical book supported by strong theoretical underpinnings. It is a useful tool for inservice workshops and personal instructional growth that teachers and staff developers will find extremely helpful. Dr. Fogarty has a knack for cutting directly to key points in an engaging style. Certainly the goal of any professional improvement plan is to eventually help learners. *How to Integrate the Curricula* can help educators assist all learners in the classroom to be thoughtful, creative, and mindful.

Dr. Heidi Hayes Jacobs
President, Curriculum Designers
Rye, New York

Acknowledgments

This book took a year—plus a lifetime—to write! The thoughts shared here represent an accumulation of ideas over time and present the core of the integrated learner model. Learners must constantly and continually make connections. As they proceed on their journeys, they single-mindedly dig into an idea and at the same time network with others for breadth across related fields. As a result, concepts come into focus and emerge as beliefs that propel learners even further along on their chosen path and into never-ending circles of expert associates. In my work with curriculum and cognitive instruction, two camps of expert associates have influenced my thinking about how to integrate the curricula: expert theorists and expert practitioners.

In the theorists' camp, I'd like to acknowledge Heidi Hayes Jacobs for providing the initial impetus for this work. Her "Design Options for an Integrated Curriculum" (in *Interdisciplinary Curriculum: Design and Implementation;* Jacobs, 1989) acted as a catalyst for the ideas presented in this book.

In addition, I am especially grateful to David Perkins for an illuminating discussion on finding fertile themes with which to integrate curricula. With his rich criteria, this thematic model takes on new integrity. In the absence of applied criteria, topical themes are often superficial, with content artificially included or excluded accordingly. David's "lenses" provide the needed rigor. In addition, thanks go to David for the idea of the characters placed in a school setting. This sparked the inclusion of the dialogues that appear throughout the book to illuminate the teachers' process as they move toward a more coherent curriculum.

Finally, also in the theorists' camp, I'd like to thank Art Costa for his initial review of the integrated models and his timely suggestion for one that illustrates how a teacher targets several ideas in a single lesson or nests several ideas together—thus, the nested Model 3.

Now, in the practitioners' camp, there are five distinct expert flanks. Influencing the first two editions of this book were teachers from Carpentersville, Illinois; the Waterford School District, in Michigan; the Richmond School District, in British Columbia, Canada; and Virginia Beach Schools, in Virginia. The final group, which influenced this latest edition, were Singaporean teachers from Teach Less, Learn More (TLLM) Ignite Schools.

Elementary and middle school teachers from Carpentersville, Illinois, worked on models to help integrate the curricula for lessons and learners. Some of their lesson designs appear as examples in this book. I thank the following teachers for their early efforts in exploring this idea of an integrated curriculum: Carol Bonebrake, Jane Atherton, Suzanne Raymond, Barbara Bengston, Al Eck, Kathleen Vehring, Roseanne Day, Nancy Blackman, Clifford Berutti, Linda Morning, Diane Gray, and Terri Pellant.

Thanks to Julie Casteel and her teachers in Michigan, especially Al Monetta, Chris Brakke, Lori Broughton, and Sue Barber, who provided the topics to fill in the first model in Figure 1.1. A pioneer practitioner leading the thinking skills movement into action research teams, Julie Casteele was on the cutting edge with the integrated learning idea. Thanks to both Julie and her risk-taking staff for letting me test the models with real teachers.

Thanks also to friends and colleagues in Canada, first to Carol-Lyn Sakata, who brought us there, then to Bruce Beairsto, David Shore, and Darlene Macklam, for introducing us to the teachers of Richmond. Their heroic efforts to implement a visionary provincial document, *Year 2000: A Framework for Learning,* inspired our work. I am especially indebted to one teacher, Heather MacLaren. She asked her seventh graders to prepare to talk at their parent conferences about what they had done that year and how all the things they had learned overlapped and were connected. The students' intricate Venn diagrams provided graphic representations of integrating the curricula as perceived through the eyes of learners. These drawings sparked our thinking about creative, integrative models.

With 80 teachers in a summer workshop in Richmond called "Teaching for Transfer," including John Barell, David Perkins, and our superhero, Captain Meta Cognition, we had a first stab at trying to help teachers sift out curricular priorities. This, too, served as an initial springboard for our ideas about how to integrate the curricula. Also, special thanks to Monica Pamer, Gina Rae, and Jacquie Anderson for their conversations and encouragement.

The fourth set of practitioners are those from the Virginia Beach Schools. Their work with student learning standards in designing performance tasks illuminates the process of designing integrated curricula with the "standards in mind." For their robust performance tasks, I am most grateful.

And for the fifth set of pioneering educators, I must salute the Singapore Ministry of Education leadership, especially Karen Lam and Puay Lim; the Academy of Principals and the efforts of Ezra Ng; and the TLLM Ignite school teams for their dedicated efforts in creating more engaged learning models with the integrated curriculum approach. Working with the 10 models, these teachers are dedicated to the development of an integrated curriculum that demonstrates richness, rigor, and integrity. We value their work immensely as it enhances ours.

I would be remiss if I neglected to mention the network of colleagues who have helped shape this book. Thanks to Jim Bellanca for his mentoring ways; Hudson Perigo for shepherding the process with skill and charm; and last but not least, our office administrator, Megan Moore, for her invaluable assistance in organizing and reorganizing, formatting and reformatting, editing and re-editing, and submitting and resubmitting. She has been a godsend in this endeavor.

PUBLISHER'S ACKNOWLEDGMENTS

Corwin gratefully acknowledges the contributions of the following reviewers:

John C. Baker
Eighth-Grade Social Studies Teacher/Department Chair
Salem Middle School
Apex, NC

Julie Prescott
Assessment Coordinator
Vallivue High School
Caldwell, ID

Darlene Vigil
Language Arts Coordinator
Albuquerque Public Schools
Albuquerque, NM

Mark White
Elementary School Principal
Hintgen Elementary School
La Crosse, WI

About the Author

**Robin Fogarty** received her doctorate in curriculum and human resource development from Loyola University of Chicago. A leading proponent of the thoughtful classroom, she has trained educators throughout the world in curriculum, instruction, and assessment strategies. She has taught at all levels from kindergarten to college, served as an administrator, and consulted with state departments and national ministries of education in the United States, Puerto Rico, Russia, Canada, Australia, New Zealand, Germany, Great Britain, Singapore, Korea, and the Netherlands. She has published articles in *Educational Leadership, Phi Delta Kappan,* and the *Journal of Staff Development.* She is the author or coauthor of numerous publications, including *Brain-Compatible Classrooms* (2009), *Literacy Matters* (2007), *The Adult Learner* (2007), *A Look at Transfer* (2007), *Close the Achievement Gap* (2007), *Twelve Brain Principles That Make the Difference* (2007), *Nine Best Practices That Make the Difference* (2007), and *From Staff Room to Classroom: A Guide for Planning and Coaching Professional Development* (2006).

Introduction

To the young mind every thing is individual, stands by itself. By and by, it finds how to join two things and see in them one nature; then three, then three thousand; and so, tyrannized over by its own unifying instinct, it goes on tying things together, diminishing anomalies, discovering roots running underground whereby contrary and remote things cohere and flower out from one stem. . . . The astronomer discovers that geometry, a pure abstraction of the human mind, is the measure of planetary motion. The chemist finds proportions and intelligible method throughout matter; and science is nothing but the finding of analogy, identity, in the most remote parts.

—Emerson

WHAT IS THIS BOOK ALL ABOUT?

To help the "young mind . . . [discover] roots running underground whereby contrary and remote things cohere and flower out from one stem" is at once the mission of the teacher and of the learner. To that end, this book presents models to connect and integrate the curricula in a more coherent fashion.

Yet the question begging for an answer is, "What does integrating the curricula mean?" Does it mean sifting out the parcels of each overloaded discipline and focusing, in depth, on the true priorities, the enduring learnings (Wiggins & McTighe, 1998) (Cellular Model)?

> Yet the question begging for an answer is, "What does integrating the curricula mean?"

Does it mean integrating or connecting yesterday's lesson to today's topic? Or relating all issues studied in the biology class to the concept of evolution? Or studying concepts such as power and isolation throughout social studies topics? Does it mean making connections explicit rather than implicit with every classroom opportunity (Connected Model)?

Does integrating curricula mean targeting multidimensional skills and concepts into one lesson (Nested Model) or mapping the curricula by rearranging the sequence of when a topic is taught to coincide with a parallel topic in another content area (Sequenced Model)? Does it mean integrating one subject with another through the learner's conceptual eye or selecting an overall theme

Model	Definition
Cellular Model	Focusing on priorities of each course
Connected Model	Making explicit connections with each classroom opportunity
Nested Model	Targeting multi-dimensional skills and concepts into one lesson
Sequenced Model	Rearranging sequence when a topic is taught to coincide with a parallel topic in another discipline
Shared Model	Integrating one subject with another through the learner's conceptual eye
Webbed Model	Weaving natural and obvious themes of a subject (such as the work of an artist or writer) into the fabric of a discipline
Threaded Model	Integrating what is taught with cognitive tools, strategies, and technical tools that cross disciplines
Integrated Model	Involving interdisciplinary team discussions when planning curriculum
Immersed Model	Connecting past experiences and prior knowledge with new information
Networked Model	Building new bonds of interest with other experts through networking

(such as persistence or argument) or a simple topic (such as transportation) to use as a "big idea" thematic umbrella (Shared Model)? Or is it more deductive in nature, such as selecting a book, an era, or an artist and weaving those natural and obvious themes into the fabric of the discipline (Webbed Model)?

Does integrating curricula mean integrating the content of what is taught with cognitive tools (predicting, classifying), cooperative strategies (debating, finding consensus), and technical tools (computer skills, electronic media) that cross disciplines and spill into real-life situations (Threaded Model)? Or does it encompass interdisciplinary team discussions and planning in which conceptual overlaps (structures, cycles) become the common focus across departments (Integrated Model)?

Does integrating the curricula mean exploiting integrative threads sparked from within the intense interests of the learner (photography, hunting, dancing) to connect past experiences and prior knowledge with new information and experiences (Immersed Model)? Or does it mean reaching out to build bonds with experts in the area of interest (hunting, environmentalist, cartographer) through networking (Networked Model)?

The answer, of course, is that integrating the curricula can be any or all—and more—of the aforementioned models. Each teacher and each learner views the integration process differently. Each finds natural and robust ways to connect the world in search of deeper meaning and richer understanding. Each seeks the relatedness between and among things to discover "roots running underground whereby contrary and remote things cohere and flower out from one stem."

WHY BOTHER?

Why bother being concerned with a coherent curriculum? What is the rationale for connecting ideas, discerning themes, and threading skills? The answer lies in the four winds of change, coming from four distinct directions, that create the urgency for a more integrated curriculum. The north and south represent the ideas of educational theorists and the challenges of practitioners; the east and west represent the concerns of parents and the perspective of students themselves. From the theorists come data on teaching, learning, and the human brain; from the practitioners, frustration with an overcrowded standards-based and test-driven curriculum. From opposite vectors, parents are concerned about student preparation and readiness for real-world issues, while students see learning as fractured and not very relevant. A closer look at these crosswinds of change reveals their impact on the current educational climate of school reform in our nation's schools.

The Theorists: Research on the Brain and Learning

Supporting the concept of a more connected, integrated curriculum is a research base that delineates 12 principles of the brain and learning (Caine & Caine, 1994, 1997). Note that some of the principles in Figure 0.1 are common sense, others reinforce accepted pedagogy, and still others are just gaining acceptance in the world of cognitive/neuroscience.

> Supporting the concept of a more connected, integrated curriculum is a research base that delineates 12 principles of the brain and learning.

---

1. Learning is enhanced by challenge and inhibited by threat.

2. Emotions are critical to patterning.

3. Learning involves both focused and peripheral perception.

4. The brain processes parts and wholes simultaneously.

5. The brain has a spatial memory system and a set of systems for rote learning.

6. The brain is a parallel processor.

7. Learning engages the entire physiology.

8. Each brain is unique.

9. Understanding and remembering occur best when the facts are embedded in natural, spatial memory.

10. The search for meaning is innate.

11. The search for meaning occurs through patterning.

12. Learning always involves conscious and unconscious processes.

Figure 0.1   Caine & Caine's 12 Principles of the Brain and Learning

SOURCE: Adapted from *Making Connections: Teaching and the Human Brain,* by R. N. Caine and G. Caine, 1994, Reading, MA: Addison-Wesley. Copyright 1994 by Geoffrey Caine. Adapted with permission.

Creating the Learning Environment

The first three principles create the learning environment.

1. *Learning is enhanced by challenge and inhibited by threat.* The brain learns optimally when appropriately challenged and reacts viscerally when it senses threat. Therefore, a safe, rich environment fosters a state of relaxed alertness for learning, whereas threatening experiences, such as testing situations, often create a state of fear and anxiety.

2. *Emotions are critical to patterning.* Emotions and cognition cannot be separated. When emotions kick in, the brain pays attention. Attention is necessary for memory and learning. Therefore, a positive emotional hook, such as an intriguing question, enhances learning.

3. *Learning involves both focused and peripheral perception.* The brain responds to the entire sensory context. Therefore, in an enriched environment, peripheral information can be purposely organized to facilitate learning. Learning centers, study stations, and even the way teachers represent information on the board are organizational tools that enhance memory and learning.

Using Explicit and Implicit Memory Systems

Principles 4 and 5 involve the memory systems.

4. *The brain processes parts and wholes simultaneously.* Bilateralization of right and left hemisphere processing, although inextricably linked for interaction, allows the brain to reduce information into parts and at the same time perceive and work with the information as a whole. Therefore, immediate application of direct instruction of skills and concepts allows the learner to perceive information from both perspectives.

5. *The brain has a spatial memory system and a set of systems for rote learning.* There are facts and skills that are dealt with in isolation and require rehearsal, and at the same time there is natural, spatial memory that needs no rehearsal and affords instant memory. Therefore, rote memorization techniques are necessary for fostering long-term learning for transfer. Rote memorization requires more conscious effort to remember because the facts may have little meaning or relevance to the learner. When the brain senses that there is no need to remember, it tends to let go of the information. Therefore, rote memorization of isolated facts often needs more explicit work to learn and recall information, whereas spatial memory has built-in cues that help in the retrieval of information. Teaching that focuses on the personal world of the learner to make learning relevant taps into the experiential or spatial memory system. In sum, rote memory is explicit, while spatial memory is implicit.

Processing Incoming Information

Processing is supported by four principles.

6. *The brain is a parallel processor.* Thoughts, emotions, imagination, and predispositions operate simultaneously. Therefore, optimal learning results

from orchestrating the learning experience to address multiple operations in the brain. When all four lobes of the brain (frontal, occipital, temporal, parietal) are activated, memory is enhanced. And memory is the only evidence we have of learning (Sprenger, 1999).

7. *Learning engages the entire physiology.* Learning is as natural as breathing, yet neuron growth, nourishment, and emotional interactions are integrally related to the perception and interpretation of experiences. Therefore, stress management, nutrition, exercise, and relaxation are integral to the teaching and learning process.

8. *Each brain is unique.* Although most brains have a similar set of systems for sensing, feeling, and thinking, the set is integrated differently in each brain. In short, each and every brain is wired differently. Therefore, teaching that is multifaceted, with inherent choices and options for the learner, fosters optimal learning.

9. *Understanding and remembering occur best when the facts are embedded in natural, spatial memory.* Specific items are given meaning when embedded in ordinary experiences, such as learning grammar and punctuation and applying that learning to writing. Experiential learning that affords opportunities for embedded learning is necessary for optimal learning.

Making Meaning

The final three principles address the brain's way of making meaning.

10. *The search for meaning is innate.* The search for meaning cannot be stopped, only channeled and focused. Therefore, classrooms need stability and routine as well as novelty and challenge. The learning can be shepherded explicitly through mediation and reflection.

11. *The search for meaning occurs through patterning.* The brain has a natural capacity to integrate vast amounts of seemingly unrelated information. Therefore, when teaching invokes integrated, thematically reflective approaches, learning is more brain compatible and, subsequently, enhanced.

12. *Learning always involves conscious and unconscious processes.* Enormous amounts of unconscious processing go on beneath the surface of awareness. Some of this happens when a person is awake, and much of it continues when a person is at rest or even asleep. Other learning occurs when the person is fully conscious and aware of the process. Therefore, teaching needs to be organized experientially and reflectively to benefit maximally from the deep processing.

Profile of Intelligences

In addition to these principles of the brain and learning, another important fact is that each brain has a unique profile of intelligences (Gardner, 1983, 1999) that reveal both strengths and weaknesses in accessing learning. These intelligences include verbal-linguistic, visual-spatial, interpersonal-social, intrapersonal-introspective, musical-rhythmic, logical-mathematical, bodily-kinesthetic, and naturalist-physical world.

> These principles of learning and the theory of multiple intelligences provide a profound backdrop of theory-embedded ideas.

These principles of learning and the theory of multiple intelligences provide a profound backdrop of theory-embedded ideas that comprise this first wind of change. What does this forceful wind bring to the educational agenda? It brings the idea of orchestrating the curriculum into complex experiences that immerse students in multiple ways of learning and knowing (Kovalic, 1993). These robust curriculum models include integrated, thematic instruction and ongoing projects and performances, such as a student-produced newspaper, a school musical, or a service learning project to eliminate graffiti in the community (Caine & Caine 1991, 1994, 1997). This seamless learning—curricula that find the "roots running underground"—fosters connection-making for lessons and learners.

The Practitioners: Abandonment of an Overloaded Curriculum and Adherence to Standards of Learning

One university professor tells his pre-med students, "By the time you graduate and become practicing physicians, 50 percent of what we've taught you will be obsolete . . . and we don't know which half that will be" (Fogarty & Bellanca, 1989). Curriculum overload is a reality that teachers from kindergarten to college face every day. Drug and alcohol education, AIDS awareness, consumer issues, marriage and family living, computer technology, Web and Internet training, wikis, blogs, podcasts, character education and bullying, the human brain, and safety and violence prevention programs have all been added over the years to an already content-packed curriculum. There is no end to it. The myriad content standards of the various disciplines and the process standards or life skills—thinking, organizing, assessing information, problem solving and decision making, cooperation, collaboration, and teamwork—inundate the expanding curriculum.

Meeting Standards With Integrated Curricula

There is much concern about how to meet the spectrum of content standards required by various states. Some think that each standard must be addressed discretely and within a particular discipline. Yet common sense tells us that if educators try to approach standards by laying them end to end in a sequential discipline-based map, they would need to add at least two more years to the schooling cycle. The only way the compendium of standards can possibly be met is by clustering them into logical bundles and addressing them in an explicit yet integrated fashion.

> Common sense tells us that if educators try to approach standards by laying them end to end in a sequential discipline-based map, they would need to add at least two more years to the schooling cycle.

It's not standards *or* curriculum, but rather standards *and* curriculum. Standards help to prioritize content teaching in an overloaded, fragmented, and sometimes outdated curriculum. They provide the foundation for what students need to know and be able to do. Well-designed standards help set the curricular priorities necessary for an integrated, coherent, and authentic curriculum.

With this solid foundation firmly in place, decisions about curriculum become seamless as teachers decide what to selectively abandon and judiciously include in their planning. Standards champion the cause of a more connected, more relevant, more purposeful curriculum at all levels of schooling.

The sample standards of learning in Figure 0.2 illustrate the types of learning goals contained in typical state standards for student achievement. A cursory look at these reveals the broad strokes of the standards and the ease of integration that can result if they are clustered and layered within robust learning.

This book promotes the concept of a standards-based and integrated curriculum that is reflective of lifelong learning. With standards as the guide for rigorous and relevant curricular decisions, readers may use the inventories provided later in this introduction (Figures 0.7 and 0.8) to determine what they are already doing to foster integration of concepts, skills, and attitudes across the disciplines.

These quick inventories introduce readers to the 10 models that shape integration of the curricula in myriad ways. As readers learn about the models described in this book, they discover ways to prioritize curriculum concerns, methods for sequencing and mapping curricular content, templates for webbing themes across disciplines, techniques for threading life skills into all content areas, and strategies to immerse students in content through self-selected, personally relevant learning experiences.

The focus on standards-based curricula begins the conversation about what students need to know and be able to do. The concept of integrated curricula continues the conversation with practical ways to transform that learning into real-life experiences that transfer effortlessly into future applications.

> The concept of integrated curricula continues the conversation with practical ways to transform that learning into real-life experiences.

Remember, it's not standards *or* integrated curriculum, but both standards *and* integrated curriculum that lead to students who are well prepared for a world that we as their teachers may never know.

With a multitude of standards as the goal, coverage of content, of course, is an ongoing concern as traditional evaluations (e.g., "the test") are supplemented with more authentic assessments (e.g., portfolios, performances). Yet as Hunter (1971) so aptly puts it, "Covering the curriculum is like taking a passenger to the airport—you rush around and get to the airport on time, but you leave the passenger at home" (p. 51). In other words, a teacher finishes the book or curriculum but wonders if the students came along for the ride. In the flurry of covering content standards to prepare students for "the test," teachers leave some students far behind. As one student said, "Mrs. Smith, may I be excused? My brain is full."

What does this powerful wind of change mean for schools? It means educators need to seek ways to "selectively abandon and judiciously include" standards in the curriculum (Costa, quoted in Fogarty, 1991, p. 65). The standards are the goals of the curriculum approach, within a single discipline, across content areas, and in the mind of the learner.

The Parents: What Will Our Children Need 25 Years From Now?

A father of a 13-year-old describes the typical, cellular model of schooling in which an eighth-grade student brings home "thirty examples to do for math

Communications Arts Standards

Students will acquire a solid foundation that includes knowledge of and proficiency in:

1. speaking and writing standard English (grammar, punctuation, spelling)

2. reading and evaluating fiction (poetry, drama) and nonfiction (biographies, newspapers, technical manuals)

3. relationships between language and culture

Mathematics Standards

Students will acquire a solid foundation that includes knowledge of and proficiency in:

1. addition, subtraction, multiplication, division, and other number sense

2. data analysis, probability, and statistics

3. mathematical systems, geometry, and number theory

Science Standards

Students will acquire a solid foundation that includes knowledge of and proficiency in:

1. properties and principles of matter and energy, force and motion

2. characteristics and interactions of living organisms

3. processes of scientific inquiry

Social Studies Standards

Students will acquire a solid foundation that includes knowledge of and proficiency in:

1. economic principles

2. principles of democracy and processes of governance

3. geographical study and analysis

Fine Arts Standards

Students will acquire a solid foundation that includes knowledge of and proficiency in:

1. processes and techniques of production, exhibition, and performance

2. principles and elements of different art forms

3. interrelationships of visual and performing arts

Health/Physical Education Standards

Students will acquire a solid foundation that includes knowledge of and proficiency in:

1. structures of, functions of, and relationships among human body systems

2. principles and practices of mental health

3. principles of movement and fitness

Figure 0.2 Sample Standards of Learning

SOURCE: Adapted from *Standards of Learning,* by Missouri Department of Elementary and Secondary Education, 1996, Jefferson City, MO: Author. Copyright 1996 by Missouri Department of Elementary and Secondary Education. Adapted with permission.

homework, twenty minutes of trombone practice, an autobiography to complete, irregular French verbs to learn for a test, and a chapter to read in the science text" (Fogarty, 1991, p. 61). He goes on: "There is a need to examine what students learn

Surely we must wonder: what do we want kids to know twenty-five years from now?

under these circumstances. Students may opt to do all of it, do some of it or do none of it. Surely we must wonder: what do we want kids to know twenty-five years from now? And, we must create the organizational structure that eliminates obstacles and enables students to grow and learn" (p. 62).

This wind of change means that students need schooling for a lifetime, not just for the test (Bellanca & Fogarty, 1991). In terms of relevant learning for life, one parent related a comment from her son, who told her, "I have a million things on my mind, and not one of them turned up on the test."

Yes, educators want all students to meet the learning standards, and they want them to pass the test, but in the end they really want students to be able to function effectively in life. Interestingly, one critical element of integrated learning is the lifelike projects that are relevant and meaningful to students.

The Students: Education Is a Vaccination

A student once told me, "Math is not science; science is not English; English is not history. A subject is something you take once and need never take again. It's like getting a vaccination; I've had my shot of algebra. I'm done with that." While subject matter content falls neatly into those discipline-based departments, students, unfortunately, do not compartmentalize themselves or their learning that readily.

Learning is incidental and inductive (Kovalic, 1993); it's holistic and interactive (Bellanca & Fogarty, 1991). Students learn complex language skills from their interactions with the language in genuine and authentic episodes. Baby talk disappears because other people do not talk that way. The comment "We learned about unregular verbs today" will be self-corrected to conform with standard English because students desperately want to say things "the right way." And they learn much of this naturally in integrated, cross-ability groupings of siblings and peers.

What does this wind of change mean? It means a shift toward more holistic, experiential learning for children. It means problem-based learning, case studies, performance tasks, service learning, apprenticeships, and internships. Learning is a function of experience, and teachers must create the experiences for learners.

HOW CAN THE CURRICULUM BE INTEGRATED?

Each teacher and each learner views the integration process differently. Yet there is a common vision encompassing three distinct dimensions that is accepted by a large number of educators (see Figure 0.3).

Each teacher and each learner views the integration process differently.

The vertical spiral represents the spiraling curricula built into most texts and standards documents as content is integrated and revisited through the K–12 grades. Introduction, development, and mastery of certain materials are expected at various levels in preparation for building on that material for the next concepts at subsequent levels. Integration occurs vertically throughout the schooling years.

The horizontal band represents the breadth and depth of learning in a given subject. As different subjects are approached, explored, and learned within each discipline, a cumulative effect is anticipated. Students are to expand their conceptual bases for future learning in related fields: one math concept builds toward the next as ideas are integrated within a discipline.

Finally, the circle represents the integration of skills, themes, concepts, and topics across disciplines as similarities are noted. These explicit connections are used to enhance the learning in a holistic manner as students link ideas within one subject area and from one subject to another. Both integration within a discipline and integration across disciplines are necessary to fully integrate the curricula.

10 Models of Integrating the Curricula

To further explore this idea, this book presents detailed discussions on a range of models (see Figure 0.4 for a graphic overview). Beginning with an exploration within single disciplines, at the left end of the spectrum, and continuing with models that integrate across several disciplines, the continuum ends with the ultimate and most natural models that integrate within the learner.

These models provide a tool for teachers and teacher leaders to inventory what they are already doing in their classrooms and schools to integrate the curricula. Figure 0.5 identifies the 10 views for integrating the curricula. See Figures 0.6 and 0.7 for interactive charts of the 10 models.

> These are the forces that are moving educators toward integrated, holistic, and authentic kinds of learning.

The winds of change are stronger than we think. The brain research, the off-loading of an overloaded curriculum, the emergence of standards-based curricula, the need for the life skills of thinking and collaborating, and the call for learner-centered schools are moving forces in the educational world today. These winds signal the need for integrated, rich, and robust curricula that serve as gateways to lifelong learning—not as gatekeepers that block the pathways from one discipline to another. These are the forces that are moving educators toward integrated, holistic, and authentic kinds of learning. The winds will not calm. Change is in the air. It is imminent.

AGREE/DISAGREE INTRODUCTORY ACTIVITY

Use the Agree/Disagree chart (Figure 0.8) to record your positions regarding statements about integrating the curricula before reading more about it. Read each statement and place a plus, minus, or question mark next to it.

Plus—Agree

Minus—Disagree

Question Mark—Not Sure

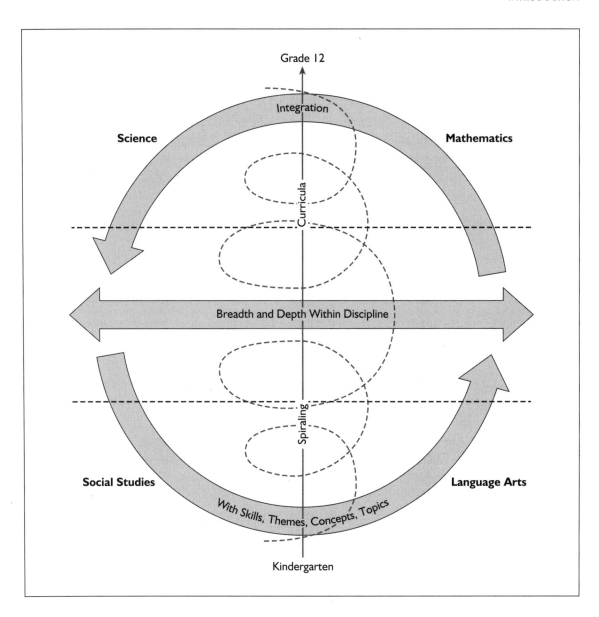

Figure 0.3 How to Integrate the Curricula: Three Dimensions

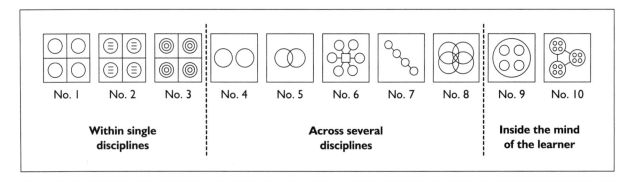

Figure 0.4 How to Integrate the Curricula

Ten Views for Integrating the Curricula: How Do You See It?

1 **Cellular**
Periscope—one direction; one sighting; narrow focus on single discipline or content area

Description
The traditional model of separate and distinct disciplines, as depicted by student learning standards in each discipline area.

Example
The teacher applies this view in mathematics, science, social studies, language arts or sciences, humanities, fine and practical arts.

2 **Connected**
Opera glass—details of one discipline; focus on subtleties and interconnections

Description
Within each subject area, course content is connected topic to topic, concept to concept, one year's work to the next, and relates ideas explicitly.

Example
The teacher relates the concept of fractions to decimals, which in turn relates to money, grades, etc.

3 **Nested**
3-D glasses—multiple dimensions to one scene, topic, or unit

Description
Within each subject area, the teacher targets multiple skills: a social skill, a thinking skill, and a content-specific skill based on standards.

Example
The teacher designs the unit on photosynthesis to simultaneously target consensus seeking (social skill), sequencing (thinking skill), and plant life cycle (science content).

4 **Sequenced**
Eye glasses—varied internal content framed by broad, related topics

Description
Topics or units of study are rearranged and sequenced to coincide with one another. Similar ideas are taught in concert while remaining separate subjects.

Example
An English teacher presents a historical novel depicting a particular period while the history teacher teaches that same historical period.

5 **Shared**
Binoculars—two disciplines that share overlapping concepts and skills

Description
Shared planning takes place in two disciplines in which overlapping concepts or ideas emerge as organizing elements.

Example
Science and mathematics teachers use data collection, charting, and graphing as shared concepts.

6 **Webbed**
Telescope—broad view of an entire constellation as one theme, webbed to the various elements

Description
Webbed curricula represent the thematic approach to integrating subject matter.

Example
The teacher presents a simple topical theme, such as the circus, and webs it to the subject areas. A conceptual theme, such as conflict, can be webbed for a broader thematic approach.

7 **Threaded**
Magnifying glass—big ideas that magnify all content through a metacurricular approach

Description
Standards, thinking skills, social skills, study skills, graphic organizers, technology, and a multiple intelligences approach to learning thread through all disciplines.

Example
The teaching staff targets prediction in reading, mathematics, and science lab experiments while the social studies teacher targets predicting current events, and thus threads prediction across all four disciplines.

8 **Integrated**
Kaleidoscope—new patterns and designs that use the basic elements of each discipline

Description
The integrated curricular model represents a cross-disciplinary approach similar to the shared model.

Example
In mathematics, science, social studies, fine arts, language arts, and practical arts, teachers look for patterns and approach content through these patterns in all the discipline areas.

9 **Immersed**
Microscope—intensely personal view that allows microscopic exploration as all content is filtered through lens of interest and expertise

Description
The individual integrates all data, from every field and discipline, by funneling the ideas through his or her area of interest.

Example
A student or doctoral candidate has an area of expert interest and sees all learning through that lens.

10 **Networked**
Prism—a view that creates multiple dimensions and directions of focus

Description
The networked model of integrated learning is an ongoing external source of input, forever providing new, extended, and extrapolated or refined ideas.

Example
An architect, while adapting the CAD/CAM technology for design, networks with technical programmers and expands her knowledge base, just as she had traditionally done with interior designers.

Figure 0.5 Toward an Integrated Curriculum

SOURCE: Based on *Design Options for an Integrated Curriculum*, by H. H. Jacobs (Ed.), 1989, Alexandria, VA: Association for Supervision and Curriculum Development.

Are We or How Are We Integrating the Curricula?

1 Cellular
Are we or how are we setting curricular priorities? (How are we managing the standards?)

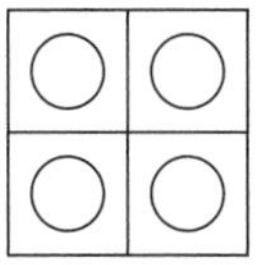

2 Connected
Are we or how are we connecting the curriculum in explicit ways? (How are we making connections—day to day, week to week, unit to unit?)

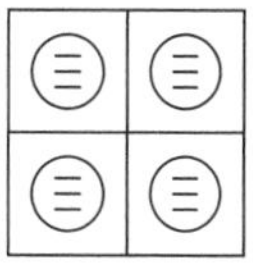

3 Nested
Are we or how are we explicitly nesting the life skills and process standards into core curricular content?

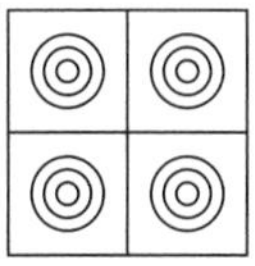

4 Sequenced
Are we or how are we aligning standards and mapping curriculum for commonsense parallels?

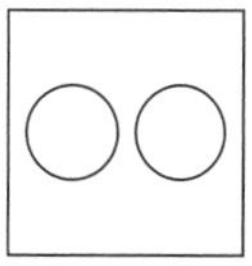

5 Shared
Are we or how are we collaborating with other teachers to find the big ideas that we share across the disciplines?

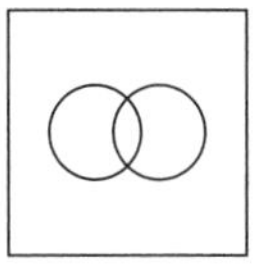

6 Webbed
Are we or how are we using patterns and themes to integrate the curricula?

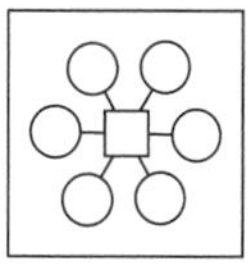

7 Threaded
Are we or how are we threading skills across the various content areas?

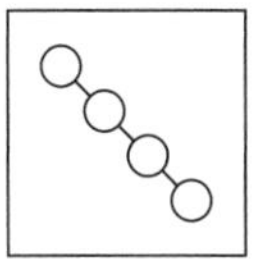

8 Integrated
Are we designing or how might we design authentic learning projects and performances that integrate a number of disciplines?

9 Immersed
Are we or how are we using learner-centered models in which students have choices?

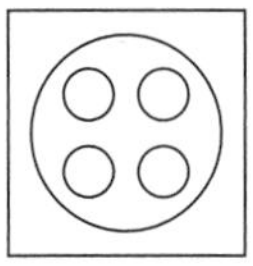

10 Networked
Are we or how are we modeling real-world learning that utilizes networks of experts?

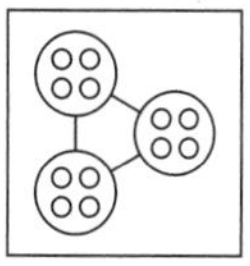

Figure 0.6 10 Models of Curricular Integration: How Are We Doing?

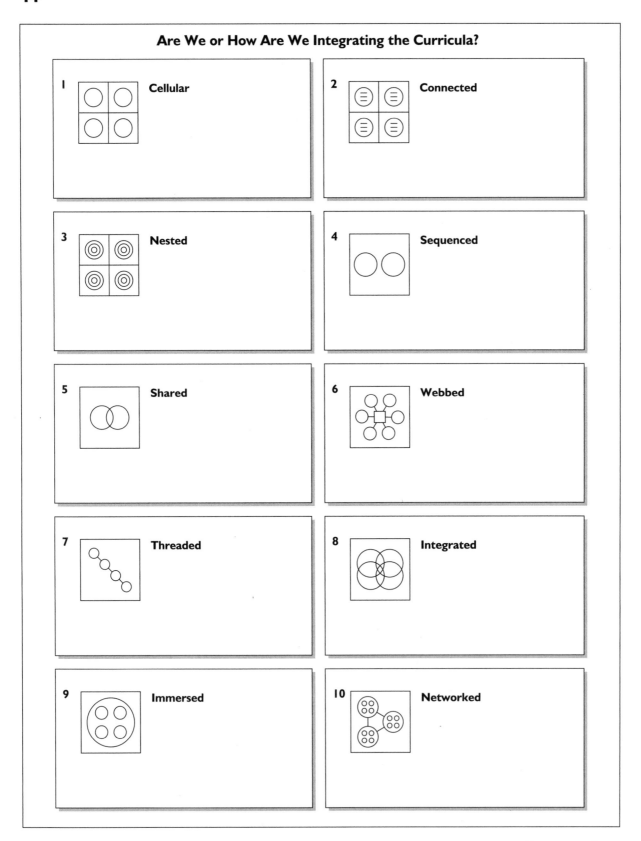

Figure 0.7   Tally Sheet for Personal Reflections and Comments

Use individual thinking first, and then dialogue with a partner.

Statement	Before		After	
	Agree	Disagree	Agree	Disagree
1. Integrating is connecting today's topics to yesterday's.				
2. Integrating means selecting an overall theme.				
3. Team teaching is part of integrating the curricula.				
4. It's so easy to integrate a novel with history.				
5. Math can't be integrated because it's sequential.				
6. *Integrated* is a synonym for *interdisciplinary*.				
7. We're already doing integrated models.				
8. The purity of the discipline is lost in integrated curricula.				
9. Integrated models are easier for students, harder for teachers.				
10. Integration is clustering standards in robust projects.				
11. Integrated models take too much time.				
12. Performance tasks are examples of integrated curricula.				

Figure 0.8   Agree/Disagree Chart

FOUR-FOLD CONCEPT DEVELOPMENT ACTIVITY

To discover the meaning behind the idea of curriculum integration, the team-building four-fold concept development activity can help the group come to a common understanding of the concept. In groups of two, three, or four, fold a large piece of poster paper into four sections and label the sections as shown in the diagram: LIST, RANK, COMPARE, ILLUSTRATE. Write "Curriculum Integration" at the top of the paper, and follow the cues provided by the headers and label in Figure 0.9.

First, brainstorm 10–20 synonyms of phrases for the concept of curriculum integration. Then, rank the top three through discussion and place the three words in the appropriate section. Now, think of an analogy, by finding a tangible, concrete object, to compare to the concept of curriculum integration.

Figures 0.10–0.12 provide several examples to use to prime the pump as you and your team think about an analogy. Look these over, and then proceed with your analogy in the third section. Then, add the accompanying visual metaphor or poster illustration in the last section.

LIST Brainstorm 20 synonyms	RANK Prioritize the top 3
COMPARE Use the analogy: _____ is like curriculum integration because both _____. 1. 2. 3.	ILLUSTRATE

Figure 0.9 Curriculum Integration

EXAMPLES OF THE FOUR-FOLD CONCEPT DEVELOPMENT ACTIVITY

CI: Curriculum Integration

LIST

Brainstorm Synonyms, Phrases, etc.

Interdisciplinary	Active Learning
Teamwork	Relationships
Connections (building)	Student-centered

Across the board

Cross subjects/departments

Prior knowledge

Themes

RANK

Best Ideas

> Interdisciplinary

> Building connections

> Active learning

COMPARE

Integrated curriculum is like a good wine _____ ,
because both _____.

1. Get better over time.
2. Leave a bittersweet taste in the mouth.
3. Provide flavor to the day.
4. Are best in moderation.

ILLUSTRATE

1998

Shiraz

CAASG

Admiralty Primary
Vineyard . . .

Figure 0.10

CI: Curriculum Integration

LIST

Brainstorm List of Synonyms, Phrases, etc.

Complement	Making meanings
Differentiated	Applying knowledge
Seamless	Enhanced learning
Projects	Infusion
Make connections	Planning
Consolidation	Teamwork
Interdisciplinary	Progressive
Reflective Practices	Interdependent learning

RANK

Best Ideas

Interdisciplinary

Infusion

Seamless

COMPARE

Concrete Object to Curriculum Integration in an Analogy

Integration is like <u>shipbuilding</u>, because both
_____.

1. Result in a greater final product.
2. Fuse different types of materials.
3. Include specialization of the different components.

ILLUSTRATE
With a Visual Metaphor

Figure 0.11

CI: Curriculum Integration

LIST

Brainstorm Synonyms, Phrases, etc.

Rich	Engaged learning
Teamwork	Relationships
Interconnected	Student-centered
Cross subjects/departments	Connectedness
Prior knowledge	Woven
Themes	Interwoven
Threaded	Laced
Coherency	Spiced
Robust	

RANK

Best Ideas

Student-centered

Connectedness

Coherency

COMPARE

Concrete Object to Curriculum Integration as an Analogy

Integration is like a bowl of ice cream, because both _____.

1. Are refreshing and renewing (quench thirst for knowledge).
2. Have many varieties and variations on the theme.
3. Are colorful (different subjects/interesting).

ILLUSTRATE
With a Visual Metaphor

Figures 0.12

HOW DO TEACHERS USE THIS BOOK?

This book is divided into 10 chapters, one for each of the models. The discussion for each model includes answers to the following questions:

What is it? (a metaphorical name and description of the model)

What does it look like? (examples of integrating the model)

What does it sound like? (examples of integrating the model)

What are the advantages? (benefits for teaching and learning)

What are the disadvantages? (detriments for teaching and learning)

When is this model useful? (purposeful and meaning applications)

To complete the discussion of each model, a vignette of teachers working with it is presented in script format for a quick readers' theater activity when using the book as a course or for the reader to ponder if using the book independently. The scripted scenarios depict the ongoing interactions and evolving journey of four faculty members trying to integrate the curricula.

There are four teachers in the scripts, symbolizing typical departmental staff who are in the process of shifting toward a more integrated approach to curriculum. The first teacher is Maria Novela, the language arts teacher, who has been with the district for 17 years. The second teacher, Sue Sum, is a recent graduate who landed a job in the mathematics department. Bob Beaker has manned his science lab for the past 5 years. And Tom Time has been in the history department "since time began." Obviously, with tongue in cheek, these scenarios are included to signify the real concerns of staff.

Each chapter ends with a set of graphics that are included for reader use. Each model includes actual samples of curricular integration for teachers to study and discuss as well as a graphic that requires teachers to design lessons and units using the construct.

Whether you are working alone, with partners, or in teams, the organizers provide immediate and visible transfer of the models into useful prototypes. In fact, a faculty can easily work with this over time to develop integrated curricula throughout the school. Each staff member or team can choose one model to work with each semester or combine models that seem to have a synergy built in. Or students themselves can work with the models to explore the connections they make within and across disciplines and within and across learners.

The templates are visible evidence of the integration ideas and solidify the ideas in a highly concrete way. As teachers begin the conversation about integrating the curricula, the spectrum of models becomes more inviting.

> As teachers begin the conversation about integrating the curricula, the spectrum of models becomes more inviting.

Model

1 Cellular

Are we or how are we setting curricular priorities?

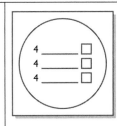

Periscope—one direction; one sighting; narrow focus on single discipline or content area.

The traditional model of separate and distinct disciplines, as depicted by student learning standards in each discipline.

Example

The teacher applies this view in mathematics, science, social studies, humanities, fine and practical arts.

"Education is the instruction of the intellect in the laws of Nature."

—Thomas Huxley

L et's not dismiss the traditional model too lightly. It has worked for many years. There must be a reason it has survived the test of time.

WHAT IS THE CELLULAR MODEL?

The traditional curricular arrangement dictates separate and distinct disciplines. Typically, the four major academic areas are labeled mathematics, science, language arts, and social studies. Fine arts and practical arts pick up other subjects, including art, music, and physical education, while technology, drafting, graphic arts, business, and accounting may be slotted in the technical arts. Another grouping of the disciplines uses the categories of humanities, sciences, practical arts, and fine arts. In the standard curriculum, these subject matter areas are more often than not taught in isolation, with no attempt to connect or integrate them. Each is seen as a pure entity in and of itself. Each has separate and distinct content standards. Although there may be overlap between physics and chemistry, the relationship between the two is implicitly, not explicitly, approached through the curriculum.

WHAT DOES IT LOOK LIKE?

In middle and high school, each discipline is taught by different teachers, in different locations throughout the building, with the students moving to different rooms. Each separate encounter carries with it a separate and distinct cellular organization, leaving students with a compartmentalized view of the curricula. A less severe cellular model, with subjects still taught separately and apart from each other, is the elementary classroom. In this situation the teacher says, "Now, put away your math books, and take out your science packets. It's time to work on our science unit." The daily schedule shows distinct time slots for mathematics, science, and social studies. Often topics from two areas are not intentionally correlated. This isolation of subjects can be the norm, even in the self-contained classroom, as content standards reign supreme.

WHAT DOES IT SOUND LIKE?

A young high school student once explained the traditional curriculum like a vaccination: "Math is not science; science is not English; English is not history. A subject is something you take once and need never take again. It's like getting a vaccination; I've had my shot of algebra. I'm done with that."

In one day, typical junior high school students may be asked to perform in seven or eight very different subjects, from mathematics to physical education. They will do this every day in addition to the homework that each subject generates. To cope with such a workload, students may have to choose between focusing on the one or two subjects they enjoy doing, and excel in them, and doing the minimum required to get by in the other subjects. Readers may wonder, "What do students learn under these circumstances? Are the needs of the system taking precedence over the needs of the students?"

WHAT ARE THE ADVANTAGES?

One of the advantages of this cellular model, of course, is that the purity of each discipline is left untainted. In addition, instructors prepare as experts in a particular field and have the luxury of digging into their subjects with both breadth and depth. This traditional model also provides a comfort zone for all concerned because it represents the norm. We're used to it. The weight of these pluses must not be taken too lightly. There is value in examining one discipline or subject as a separate and distinct entity in order to reveal the critical attributes of each discrete field. In fact, each discipline is a way of thinking that is inherent and tailored to its field. For example, mathematicians have distinct ways of categorizing problems, while literature aficionados glory in their various genres. Each and every discipline offers rigor in its way of thinking about the world, and immersion in the various disciplines has immense benefits in rounding out the spectrum of thinking for learners of all ages.

This model, although it appears at first to be somewhat fragmented, does indeed provide clear and discrete views of each discipline. In turn, the model affords a particular way of thinking, through the qualities of designated disciplines, that enhances the perspectives of learning. In addition, experts can easily sift out the priorities of their own subject areas as they live and breathe with their passion for their subject matter. In the final analysis, students are able to realize the true benefits of this cellular model when working with a mentor.

WHAT ARE THE DISADVANTAGES?

The disadvantages are threefold. First, learners are left to their own resources in terms of making connections and integrating similar concepts. Second, overlapping concepts, skills, and attitudes are not illuminated for the learner; thus, transfer of learning to novel situations is less likely to occur. To leave the learner unattended in making connections both within and across disciplines is to overlook some of the latest research on transfer of learning, which calls for explicit shepherding of the transfer with hugging and bridging strategies. Third, in this discipline-based model, students can easily get caught in an avalanche of work. Although each teacher assigns a reasonable amount, the cumulative effect can become overwhelming for students.

WHEN IS THIS CELLULAR MODEL USEFUL?

The cellular model is a useful curricular configuration in a number of cases. It works for large schools with diverse populations because these schools may offer a variety of courses that provide a spectrum of subjects to target special interests. It is also useful, of course, at the university level, where students travel on specialized paths of study that require expert knowledge for instructing, mentoring, coaching, and collaborating. This model is also helpful in teacher education programs, as the preparation can be more focused. And it is a good model for practicing teachers who want to sift out curricular priorities in order to manage the abundance of content standards as they prepare cross-departmental models for interdisciplinary planning.

Figures 1.1–1.3 are examples of completed cellular model integration exercises, and Figure 1.4 provides the opportunity for readers to record their own design for this model.

Model 1: Cellular

Readers' Theater

"On My Own"

Narrator

Meanwhile, back at the school, teachers with periscopic vision are unintentionally burying their students with homework as they individually plan their curricula . . .

Maria Novela, Language Arts

Students can rent the movie *Romeo and Juliet* over the weekend. They will be familiar with the plot, and on Monday we can focus on the beauty of Shakespearean English.

Tom Time, History

This list of topics will help students select their semester projects on Western Civilization. They can start researching their projects this weekend.

Sue Sum, Mathematics

If we get through this lesson today, I'll assign these theorems for weekend homework.

Bob Beaker, Science

Students can read the chapter on the periodic table of elements over the weekend. It's long, but then they'll have a jump on the rest of the semester.

HOW TO INTEGRATE THE CURRICULA WORKING WITH MODEL 1: CELLULAR

Essential Reasoning:

> *"I prioritize the fundamental or basic understandings first; then I look for the topics, concepts, or units that can be given a different weight."*

To work with Model 1, the Cellular Model, think about the elements of the curriculum. First, select one subject (math, science, social studies) that you teach at the elementary level or one class prep (algebra, geometry, trigonometry) that you have at the middle or high school level.

Once you have a focus on the subject or prep, think about the curriculum standards addressed, and list all of the relevant topics of study for that area.

After you have listed the topics of study, think about which ones are most important and which are least important. Then prioritize the list by numbering the items, with 1 as most important and the highest number as least important. This process is known as a forced ranking, but it is helpful to discern the significance of each topic.

After you have made your decisions, dialogue with a partner in the same department or a similar grade level about the curricular priorities in that discipline. Discuss how you set priorities and what considerations you make in deciding how to weigh the various pieces of the targeted curriculum. Let your partner comment on your list.

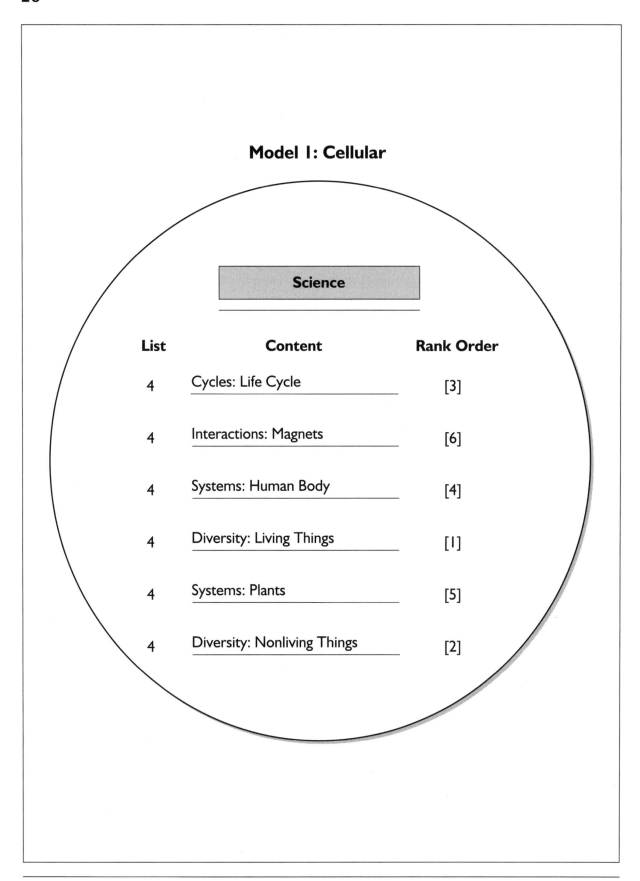

Figure 1.1 Elementary School Example

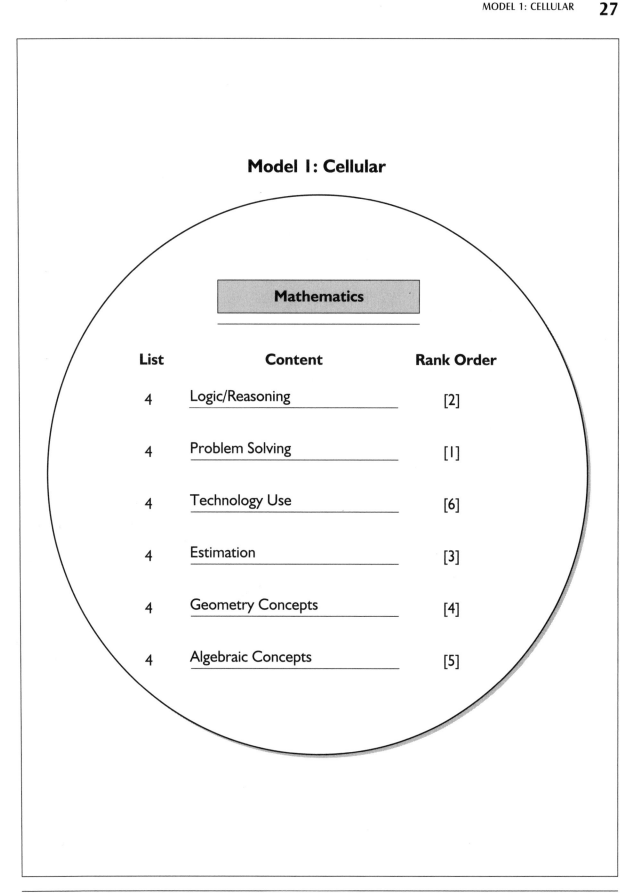

Figure 1.2 Middle School Example

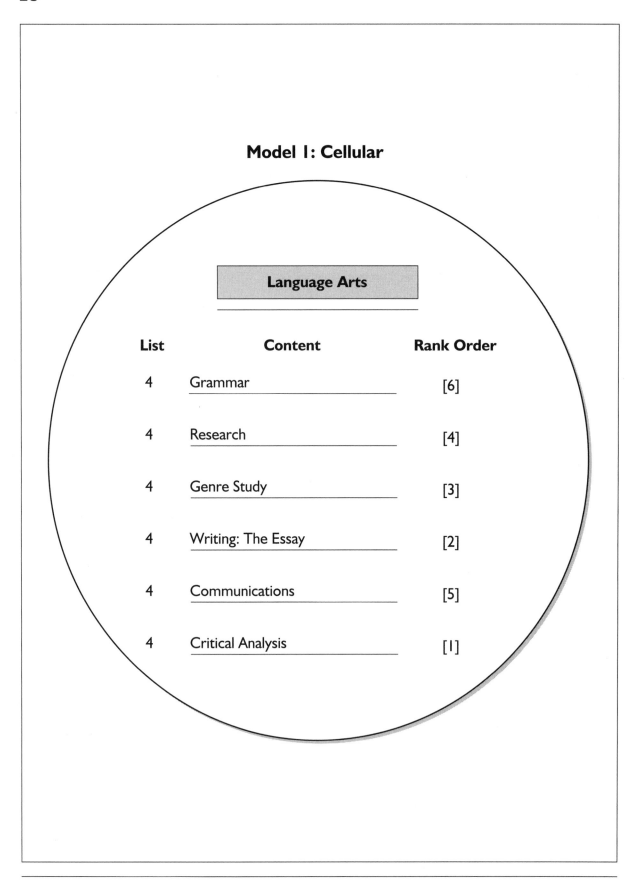

Model 1: Cellular

Language Arts

List	Content	Rank Order
4	Grammar	[6]
4	Research	[4]
4	Genre Study	[3]
4	Writing: The Essay	[2]
4	Communications	[5]
4	Critical Analysis	[1]

Figure 1.3   High School Example

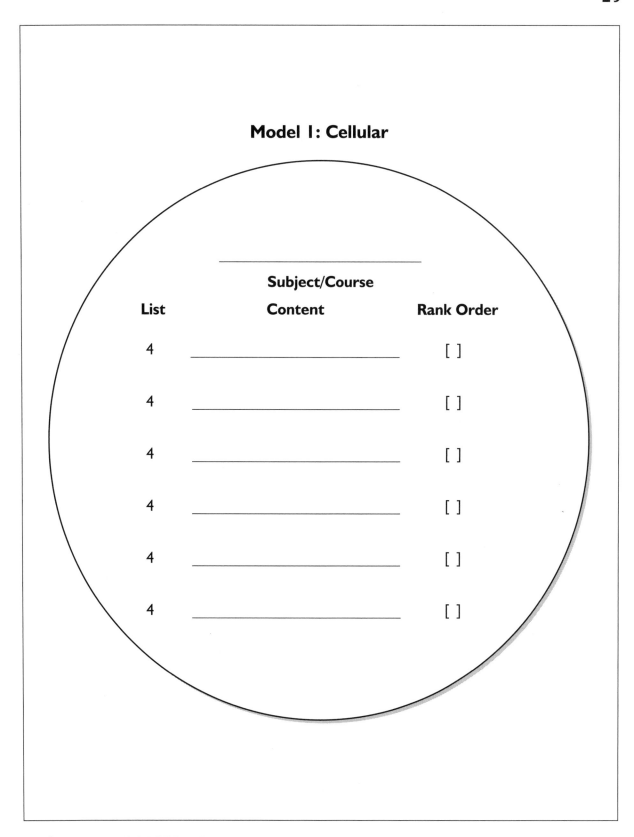

Model 1: Cellular

Subject/Course

List	Content	Rank Order
4	_____	[ ]
4	_____	[ ]
4	_____	[ ]
4	_____	[ ]
4	_____	[ ]
4	_____	[ ]

Figure 1.4   On Your Own

Notes & Reflections
Model 1: Cellular

Essential Reasoning:

"I prioritize the fundamental or basic understandings first; then I look for the topics, concepts, or units that can be given a different weight."

Each teacher in each discipline plans the topics and content in isolation from the other teachers in other disciplines. For example, the language arts teacher and the science teacher simultaneously list their traditional topics for a semester, yet they do so independently of the other disciplines.

This cellular model is truly the traditional way of working with curriculum, with little or no attention to integrating the disciplines. Yet the sequence and time allotment determined by each individual teacher, using individual criteria, is a necessary step in sifting out curricular priorities. It is the first step in how teachers set about "selectively abandoning" or "judiciously including" (Costa, 1991a, p. 65) material in curricular design.

"In third-grade math, I prioritize mathematical operations as the fundamental or basic understandings first; then I look at geometry and probabilities because I can give them a different weight in the grand scheme of things."

Connected

How are we connecting the curriculum in explicit ways?

Opera glass—details of one discipline; focus on subtleties and interconnections

Within each subject area, course content is connected topic to topic, concept to concept, one year's work to the next, and relates ideas explicitly.

Example

The teacher relates the concept of fractions to decimals, which in turn relates to money, grades, etc.

"The object of education is to prepare the young to educate themselves throughout their lives."
—Robert Maynard Hutchins

WHAT IS THE CONNECTED MODEL?

Although the major discipline areas remain separate, this curricular model focuses on making explicit connections within each subject area, connecting one topic to the next, connecting one concept to another, connecting one skill to a related skill, connecting one day's work to the next, or even connecting one semester's ideas to the next. The key to this model is the deliberate effort to relate curricula within the discipline rather than assuming that students understand the connections automatically.

In this way, students are aware of the flow of content created by the teacher. This flow enhances the connectivity between the various topics presented. It exposes the teacher's inherent planning and intentions as students become privy to the purposeful flow of the curricular elements and how they unfold in a logical sequence. More often than not, this flow is devised by the teacher for specific reasons.

WHAT DOES IT LOOK LIKE?

Within the elementary curriculum, for example, a relationship is drawn between the rock unit and the simple machines unit as students explicitly connect these while simultaneously seeing them as two distinct science areas: one is earth science and the other is physical science. By labeling for students the broad terms (in this case, earth science and physical science), teachers can help students begin to define the spectrum of the sciences for themselves with these traditional, organizational umbrellas. This becomes a first critical step in their understanding and conceptualization of the sciences as a realm of knowing.

Likewise, in a middle or secondary school setting, the earth science teacher relates the geology unit to the astronomy unit by associating the evolutionary nature of each. The similarities between the two units become organizers for students as they work through both units to see that they can make explicit interrelationships.

WHAT DOES IT SOUND LIKE?

Students see connections between subject areas that have traditionally been taught separately. For example, a student concludes that a particular law in physics has logical inconsistencies. Then he notices that when he looks at biology, he encounters that law again and once again finds logical contradictions. By looking across disciplines, he finds specific examples that he connects to support his thoughts about this particular law. The teacher can facilitate such connections in students' thinking by explicitly making links between various subject areas that occur within a single discipline. For who better to understand and explain the connections among the sciences than the science teacher?

WHAT ARE THE ADVANTAGES?

By connecting ideas within a single discipline, learners have the advantages of seeing the big picture as well as engaging in focused study of one aspect. Students see an all-encompassing picture rather than a narrow one. In addition, key skills and concepts, such as the scientific method or observation and inference, are developed over time for deeper internalization by learners. Connecting ideas within a discipline permits learners to review, reconceptualize, edit, and assimilate ideas gradually, with more chance of facilitating transfer.

WHAT ARE THE DISADVANTAGES?

The various disciplines in this model remain separated and appear unrelated, yet connections are made explicit within the designated discipline. Teachers are not encouraged to work together in this model, so content remains the focus without stretching concepts and ideas across other disciplines. The concentrated efforts to integrate within the discipline overlook opportunities to develop more global relationships to other subjects.

WHEN IS THIS CONNECTED MODEL USEFUL?

The connected model is useful as a beginning step toward an integrated curriculum. Teachers feel confident looking for connections within their own discipline. As they become adept at relating ideas within one discipline, it becomes easier to scout for connections across multiple disciplines. This process of connecting ideas applies to content standards also. It is one way that teachers manage and make sense of the overwhelming number of standards. Connection making can be done collaboratively within department meetings—which is old and familiar ground that sets a safe climate for change. Using this model to start teacher teams within a department or grade level can be a fruitful strategy to prime the pump for using more complex integration models later on.

Figures 2.1–2.3 are examples of completed connected model integration exercises, and Figure 2.4 provides the opportunity for readers to record their own design for this model.

Model 2: Connected

Readers' Theater

"The Glue"

Narrator

Back at school, our teachers start to explore the connectors within their own subject areas.

Sue Sum

I want to present units so they make more sense to students. It seems logical to introduce the concept of negative numbers after they work with the quadrants in graphing.

Bob Beaker

To help students understand how everything in biology is related to the theory of evolution, I'll have them keep an evolution notebook. They can log ideas as we study, read about, and discuss various topics.

Maria Novela

To generate an integrated understanding of American literature, I'll ask students to critique each author we read this semester using "the American Dream" as a theme. This will weave a common strand throughout the units.

Tom Time

By intertwining the unit on early Greece with Greek drama, I can help students get a study of humanities rather than discrete studies of history and literature. It should provide a more enduring image of the era.

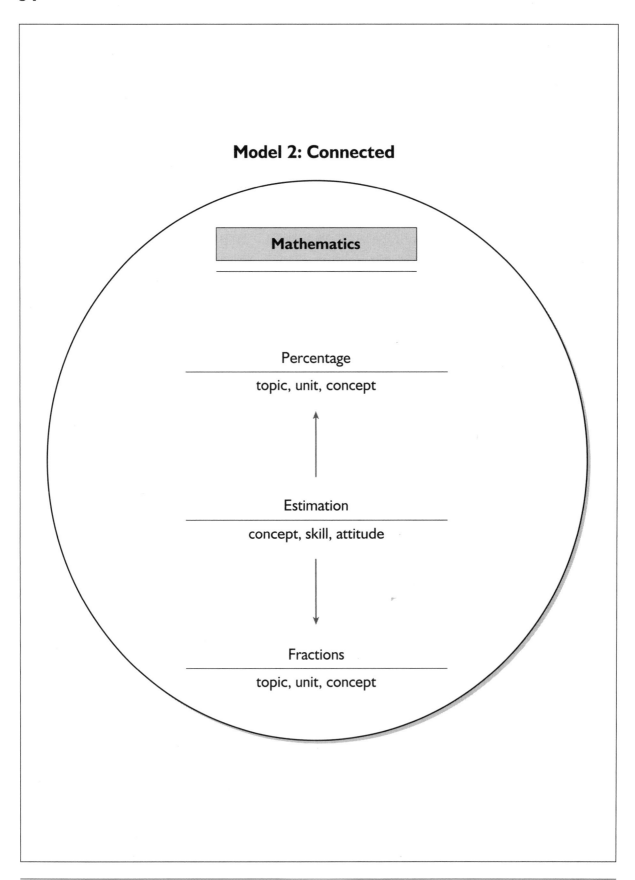

Figure 2.1 Elementary School Example

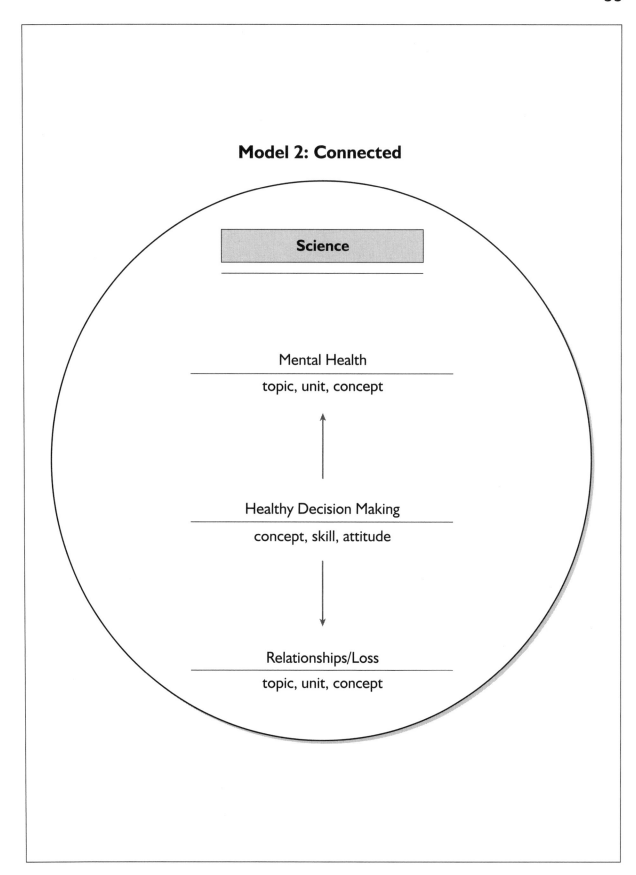

Figure 2.2 Middle School Example

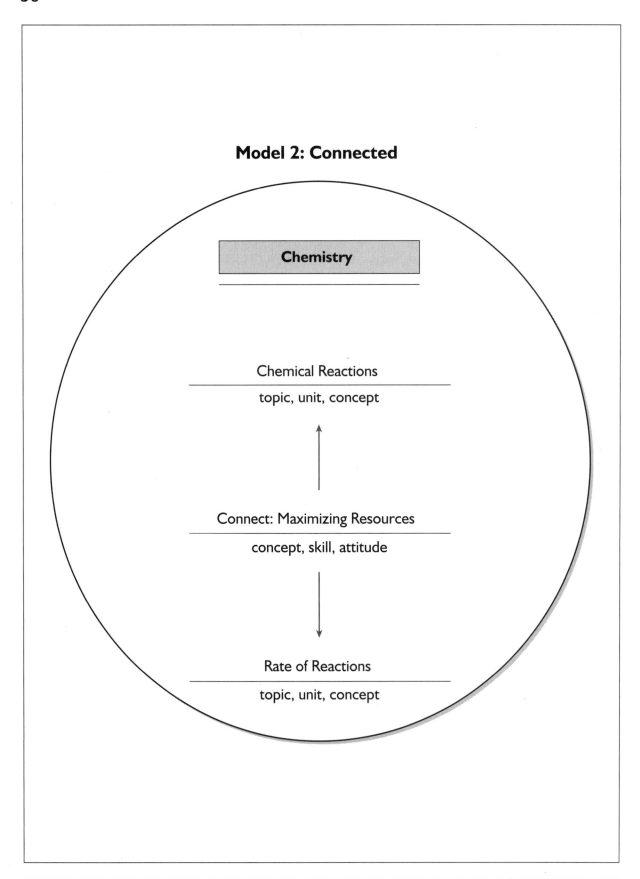

Figure 2.3   High School Example

HOW TO INTEGRATE THE CURRICULA WORKING WITH MODEL 2: CONNECTED

Essential Reasoning:

"The reason I like to teach _____ followed by _____ is because _____."

To use Model 2 to make connections between topics (or concepts or units) more explicit, identify two topics that you teach in a certain sequence, within a discipline or class. Using the template for Model 2 (Figure 2.4), put one topic on the top line and another on the bottom line to represent the one that you teach first and the one that follows.

For a logical reason, one is always taught before the other. Why? Think about why you put them together in that particular sequence. Why does it seem to make sense for you to teach these two topics in this order? And what is the connector that ties them together in this logical sequence? Now, with thought and care, put that connecting idea on the center line. Sometimes this connector is elusive. Think of the big ideas that often connect the skills, processes, attitudes, or dispositions.

Notes & Reflections

Model 2: Connected

Essential Reasoning:

"The reason I like to teach _____ followed by _____ is because _____."

Teachers in the various disciplines or subject areas delineate the flow of topics that they use as they plan particular topics, units, or concepts. As they look at the planned flow of the content, they think about their reasons for plotting the flow from one topic to the other. As they become clear on the reasons for flowing the topics, concepts, or units in their usual way, they begin to realize that there are big ideas that act as connectors or organizing threads to tie the topics together.

While teachers may have an awareness about these connecting ideas, many times students are not aware of how the curriculum ties together. But if these connections are made explicit in the minds of teachers, they can in turn share these reasons for the flow of ideas with students.

A teacher may say, "The reason I like to teach the unit on relationships followed by the one on mental health in seventh-grade health class is because they are connected by the idea of self-esteem. Many times, meaningful relationships often require sound decision making that comes from a healthy sense of self. This idea of good self-esteem is directly connected to reactions in relationships, during good times and bad. These two units just seem to go together, so it makes sense to flow them together."

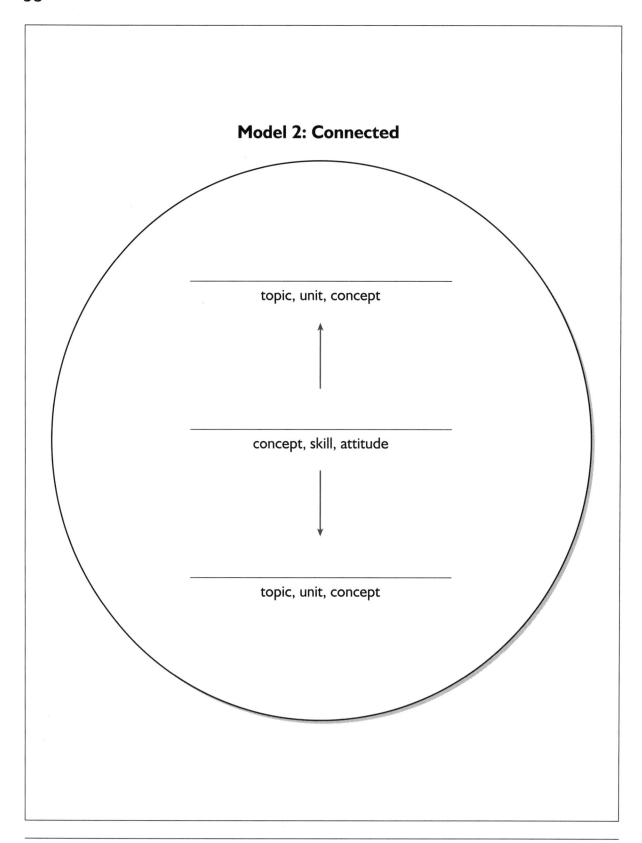

Model 2: Connected

topic, unit, concept

concept, skill, attitude

topic, unit, concept

Figure 2.4 On Your Own

Nested

*How are we explicitly nesting
life skills and process standards
into core curricular content?*

3-D glasses—multiple dimensions to one scene, topic, or unit.	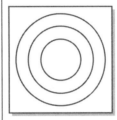 Within each subject area, the teacher targets multiple skills: a social skill, a thinking skill, and a content-specific skill based on standards. **Example** The teacher designs the unit on photosynthesis to simultaneously target consensus seeking (social skill), sequencing (thinking skill), and plant life cycle (science content).

*"The business of education is not to make the young perfect in any
one of the sciences, but to open and dispose their minds as may best
make them capable of any, when they shall apply themselves to it."*

—John Locke

WHAT IS THE NESTED MODEL?

The nested model of integration is a rich design used by skilled teachers. They know how to get the most mileage from any lesson. Yet in this nested approach to instruction, careful planning is needed to structure multiple targets and multiple standards for student learning. Nested integration takes advantage of natural clusters and combinations, so the model offers efficiency in addressing myriad skills at once.

WHAT DOES IT LOOK LIKE?

An elementary- or primary-level content lesson on the circulatory system targets the concept of *systems* as well as facts and understanding on the circulatory system in particular. But in addition to this conceptual target, the teacher highlights a thinking skill or a process standard such as cause and effect. In this scenario, throughout the study of the circulatory system, students will focus on causes and effects as they pertain to the circulatory system.

In addition, a social skill such as cooperation may be a focal point as the class learns about working with others and the skills of teamwork. Flow-chart design may be an organizational skill developed during this unit. In this highly utilized model, as the teacher covers the content standards, generic, generalized life skills are nested together to enhance the learning experience. Figure 3.1 lists examples of skills that may be targeted for nesting.

A high school lesson in a computer science class may target computer-aided design/computer-aided manufacturing (CAD/CAM) programs. Yet as the students learn the actual workings of the programs, the teacher also targets the thinking skill of visualizing for explicit exploration and practice. In this nested approach, students are also instructed in ergonomics as they design furniture for schools of the future. Thus, the teacher clusters several skills and/or process standards in this nested model of integrating the curricula.

WHAT DOES IT SOUND LIKE?

STUDENT 1:   Teachers used to be pretty predictable. They would tell you what you were supposed to know, and they tested you on it.

STUDENT 2:   Yeah! I know what you mean. It was easy to psych out the test questions because the stuff was repeated 18 times in class.

STUDENT 1:   But now they expect you to sort out what's important. And they want you to tell them how you figure things out.

Thinking skills	Social skills	Standards	Graphic organizers

• predicting
• inferring
• comparing/
  contrasting
• classifying
• generalizing
• hypothesizing
• prioritizing
• visualizing
	• attentive listening
	• clarifying
	• paraphrasing
	• encouraging
	• accepting ideas
	• disagreeing
	• summarizing
	• affirming
		• science standard:
		  inquiry
		• math standard:
		  analysis of data
		• history standard:
		  democratic process
		• language arts
		  standard:
		  expository writing
		• art standard: appreciate
		  art forms
			• web
			• Venn
			• concept map
			• flow chart
			• fishbone
			• thought tree
			• double bubble
			• priority ladder

Figure 3.1   Skills Chart

STUDENT 2: That's not all. My teacher watches our social behavior, too. She says our thinking and our behavior are just as important as our answers. This is getting out of control.

STUDENT 1: Yeah! They're getting too much mileage out of one lousy lesson.

WHAT ARE THE ADVANTAGES?

The pluses of the nested model are obvious to the veteran teacher. By nesting and clustering a number of skills and standards in the learning experience, teachers enrich and enhance student learning. Typically focusing on content, thinking strategies, social skills, and other serendipitous ideas, the single lesson takes on multiple dimensions. In this age of information overload, overcrowded curricula, numerous standards, and tight schedules, experienced teachers may seek out fertile lessons that lay the groundwork for learning in multiple areas. While the nested model provides needed attention to several areas of interest at once, it does not require the added burden of finding time to work and plan with other teachers. With this model, a single teacher can provide extensive integration of curricula. Of course, if teachers plan or work together, this model offers many opportunities to combine various and sundry skills and concepts to achieve more complexity and depth in the lessons.

WHAT ARE THE DISADVANTAGES?

The disadvantages of the nested model arise from its very nature. Nesting two, three, or four learning targets and/or standards in a single lesson may confuse students if the nesting is not executed carefully and if the combinations are superficial or artificial. The conceptual priorities of the lesson may become obscure because students are directed to perform many learning tasks at once. One other drawback of the nested model is that the teacher may not be explicit about the various layers of learning, resulting in little actual transfer or application of skills and concepts.

WHEN IS THIS NESTED MODEL USEFUL?

The nested model is most appropriate to use as teachers try to infuse process standards, such as thinking skills, cooperative skills, and literacy skills, into their content lessons. Keeping the content objectives in place while adding a thinking focus, targeting social skills, and infusing literacy skills enhances the overall learning experience. Nesting particular skills in these three areas integrates concepts and attitudes easily through structured activities. In fact, this model is commonly found in early-level classrooms, as teachers are responsible for the entire curriculum.

Figures 3.2–3.4 are examples of completed nested model integration exercises, and Figure 3.5 provides the opportunity for readers to record their own design for this model.

Model 3: Nested
Readers' Theater

"Multitasking"

Narrator

Meanwhile, back at school, our teachers are getting a lot of mileage out of their lessons—they're targeting social skills, thinking skills, and content skills within a single lesson.

Tom Time

I like the idea of nested skills as a way to integrate. It keeps my discipline pure and intact, yet I extend the lesson into other realms. In global studies, I can use De Bono's (1985) *Six Thinking Hats* for point-of-view of current events. With a jigsaw model, I can talk about student responsibility.

Bob Beaker

Good idea, Tom! When I introduce the periodic table of elements, I could focus on the content of the chart and then try nesting other skills and concepts such as patterns or memory techniques.

Maria Novela

While teaching *The Old Man and the Sea,* I can focus on author style and use of language as I have in the past. But I can also target the concepts of perseverance and friendship. Emphasizing teamwork as a social skill looks possible, too.

Sue Sum

In a math lesson, I can teach the skill of graphing information and also emphasize prediction of the line. I could use the idea of nesting and require group consensus for predictions.

HOW TO INTEGRATE THE CURRICULA WORKING WITH MODEL 3: NESTED

Essential Reasoning:

> *"I like to 'nest' several critical life skills, such as ____, ____, and _____, into the target concept of _____ because it is an easy and effective way to integrate the curricula."*

Use the template for this model (Figure 3.5) to integrate the curricula within a single discipline or class subject. The template is a bull's eye or target. Beginning with the standard of learning, place the targeted content focus in the center of the template. This is an essential learning that becomes the centerpiece of learning. Then add at least two outer circles, and nest in several process standards to illustrate graphically how you are able to layer, cluster, and combine a number of standards

Model 3: Nested

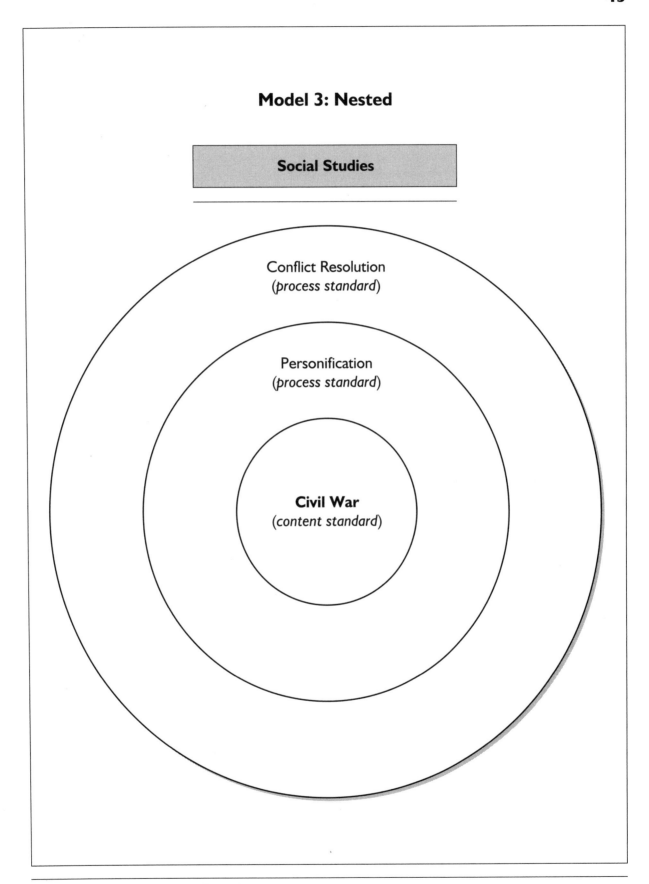

Social Studies

Conflict Resolution
(*process standard*)

Personification
(*process standard*)

Civil War
(*content standard*)

Figure 3.2   Elementary School Example

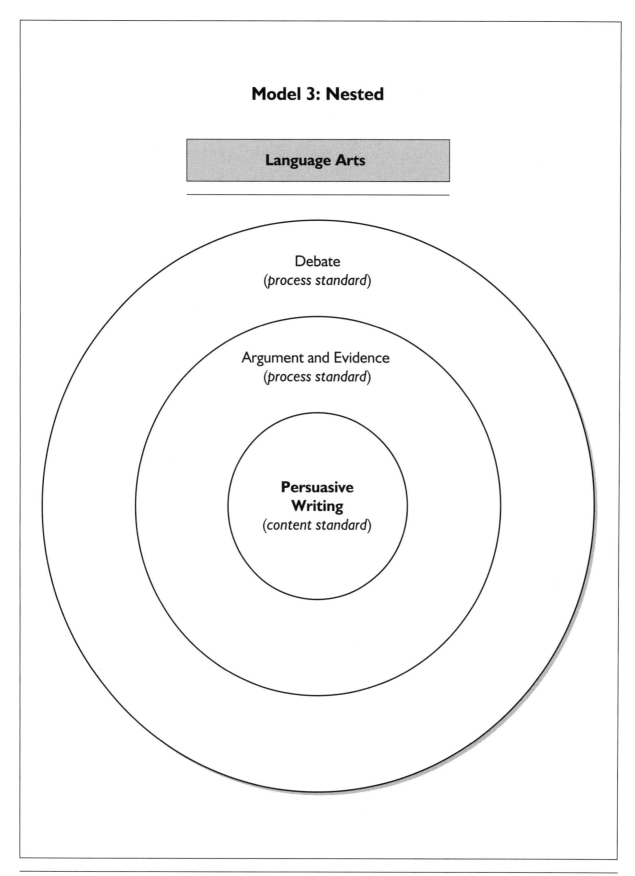

Model 3: Nested

Language Arts

Debate
(*process standard*)

Argument and Evidence
(*process standard*)

**Persuasive
Writing**
(*content standard*)

Figure 3.3 Middle School Example

Model 3: Nested

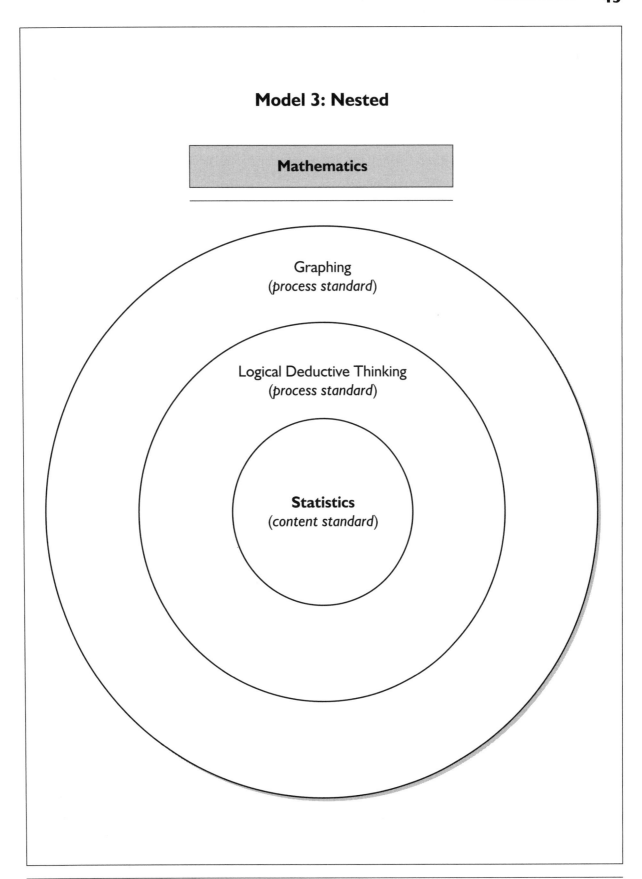

Figure 3.4   High School Example

into a robust learning experience. These process standards may be thinking skills, cooperative skills, multiple intelligences, habits of mind, technology tools, or simply other subject area tools such as reading, writing, speaking, or listening.

The following is an example of the nested model for a science unit on matter and energy:

1. Thinking skill: Compare and contrast types of energy

2. Social skill: Come to agreement about the most efficient types of energy

3. Multiple intelligences: Bodily-kinesthetic—use lab experiments to check hypotheses

4. Technology skill: Write up a lab report using Microsoft Word

5. Habit of mind: Curiosity—reflect on how curiosity is a catalyst for scientific discoveries

Notice that there are five nested areas in this example, yet they involve skills and strategies that are implicitly included in the actual orchestration of the lesson. Using the template for the nested model makes the focus on these peripheral skills and strategies explicit. The nested integration model allows teachers to see graphically and visually how lessons become richer and more robust.

Notes & Reflections
Model 3: Nested

Essential Reasoning:

"I like to 'nest' several critical life skills, such as ____, ____, and _____, into the target concept of _____ because it is an easy and effective way to integrate the curricula."

Upon reflecting on this model, it seems quite natural and fairly easy to look for the life skills that surround the development of the lesson or unit. The content is always the target focus, of course, yet there are so many opportunities to enrich the lesson with these complementary skills. It is something that many of us already do, but this nested model makes the inclusion of these supplementary skills more explicit.

Within a content standard, the teacher uses the subject matter as the pivot point for a number of skills, concepts, and attitudes. The topic or unit provides the vehicle to carry along learning in related areas.

The nested model truly is an enriching model for integrating any number of skills and attitudes, dispositions, or habits of mind into the focus lesson. Now that this model is clearer, it seems almost impossible to teach the lesson without nesting.

Think about it. To teach the lesson without nesting in these rich and rigorous skills would really be the bare-bones basics. And nesting is almost an essential integration piece if teachers expect to teach all of the life skills explicitly and effectively. Otherwise, they would simply be using the skills but not expressly teaching students about them.

Teachers often see themselves using the nested model almost daily as they understand more fully the impact of nesting skills into a content-focused lesson. After all, the apparent benefit to students in obvious.

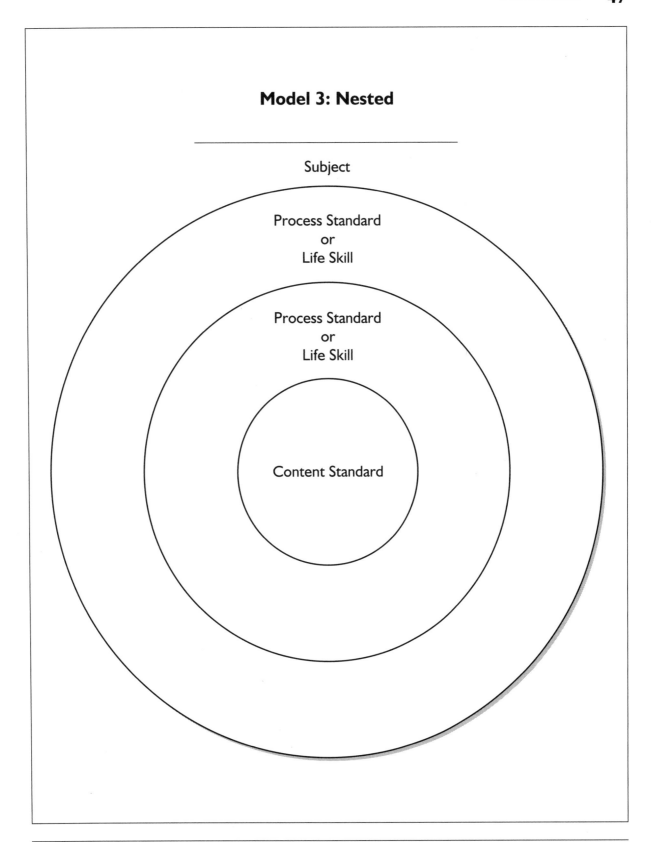

Model 3: Nested

Subject

Process Standard
or
Life Skill

Process Standard
or
Life Skill

Content Standard

Figure 3.5 On Your Own

4 Sequenced

*How are we aligning
standards and mapping curriculum
for commonsense parallels?*

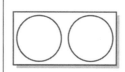

Eyeglasses—varied internal content framed by broad, related topics

Topics or units of study are rearranged and sequenced to coincide with one another. Similar ideas are taught in concert while remaining separate subjects.

Example

An English teacher presents a historical novel depicting a particular period while the history teacher teaches that same historical period.

"Education is the transmission of civilization."
—Will and Ariel Durant

WHAT IS THE SEQUENCED MODEL?

With limited articulation across disciplines, teachers can rearrange the order of their topics so that similar units coincide with each other. Two related disciplines may be sequenced so that the subject matter content of both is taught in parallel. By sequencing the order in which topics are taught, teachers allow the activities of each to enhance the understanding of the other. In essence, one subject carries the other and vice versa.

If a district or school has not done any curriculum mapping, this model provides a tool with which to begin the process. If the district or school has done some curriculum mapping by grade level or department, the next step is to begin the conversation across two subject areas that seem most likely to have connections; for example, math and science or literature and history are typical pairings. Or a teacher may pair up with a friend and colleague in the building to try mapping and resequencing some topics or units that seem like natural mates. This facilitates connection making for learners in both subject areas and reinforces deep learning as it enhances the two curricular topics under study. While this is a simple step in the integration models, it does indeed begin the process of teacher collaborations and those critical conversations about curricular content.

WHAT DOES IT LOOK LIKE?

In the self-contained elementary classroom, the book *Charlotte's Web* can accompany a unit on insects and spiders, in particular. *Johnny Tremain,* a book set during the Revolutionary War, can parallel the traditional study of that era in American history. Or the graphing unit can coincide with data collection in the weather unit.

A high school teacher might sequence the study of the stock market in mathematics with the study of the Great Depression in history. Domestic and global events can be used to parallel various units in different subjects. In this way, current relevant topics become the catalyst to study historic foundations, related mathematical concepts, or appropriate literary references.

WHAT DOES IT SOUND LIKE?

John Adams once said, "The textbook is not a moral contract that teachers are obliged to teach—teachers are obliged to teach children." Unfortunately, more often than one cares to admit, teachers may closely follow the format of the texts, going from the front of the book to the back, or try to teach each standard separately. Although this may work well in some cases, in other cases it might make more sense to rearrange the sequence of the units. The new sequence may be more logical if it parallels subject matter content across disciplines. When learners are given the advantage of seeing these natural connections across content, both the students and the teachers benefit. Learning becomes more generalized and therefore more easily transferred.

WHAT ARE THE ADVANTAGES?

By rearranging the sequence of topics, chapters, and units, teachers can dictate curricular priorities rather than follow the sequence established by the textbook's editorial staff. In this way, teachers can make critical decisions about content. From the students' point of view, the deliberate sequencing of related topics across disciplines helps them make sense of their studies in both subject and content areas. Once again, integration aids transfer. When students see teachers making similar points in different content areas, in different rooms, during different class periods, their learning is reinforced in powerful and meaningful ways. Students then have the advantage of focusing explicit attention on these learnings across subject areas, and the ideas are naturally reinforced in the different classes.

WHAT ARE THE DISADVANTAGES?

One drawback of sequenced curricula is the compromise required to shape the model. Teachers must give up autonomy in making curriculum sequences as they partner with others. Also, sequencing according to current events requires ongoing collaboration and extreme flexibility on the part of all content area teachers who are involved. This is not as easy as it sounds. However, in a very short time, even with only one afternoon together, teacher partners can usually manage to do some rearranging and sequencing as a beginning step. If this first attempt at correlating two subject areas works, the two teachers often feel encouraged to try sequencing more units for parallel teaching.

WHEN IS THIS SEQUENCED MODEL USEFUL?

This model is useful in the beginning stages of the integration process, using two discipline areas that are easily tied to each other. Working as partners, teachers start by listing curricular content separately. Then, the team juggles the separate content pieces until the two can match up or sequence some things to coincide. Then they try to parallel their different content to make more sense to the students who are learning both. In this model, both disciplines stay pure. Specific emphasis is still in the domain of the subject matter, but the students reap the benefits of related content.

In addition, the sequenced model is useful, as mentioned earlier, for starting the conversation across disciplines and subject areas. In elementary schools, classroom teachers can use this model to work with special area teachers. A classroom teacher can work with the music teacher, art teacher, physical education teacher, or special educators, such as the reading teacher or learning disabilities teacher.

At the middle and high school levels, of course, teachers can reach across two content areas. The conversation is as important as the final product in a pairing such as this because in talking to each other, teachers learn about each other's content. Once they gain this awareness, it is easy to make connections to other subject areas in order to help students see the cohesiveness.

Figures 4.1–4.3 are examples of completed sequenced model integration exercises, and Figure 4.4 provides the opportunity for readers to record their own design for this model.

Model 4: Sequenced

Readers' Theater

"Common Sense"

Narrator

By now, teachers at school are beginning to see the advantages of making connections for both lessons and learners. Our teachers start talking about doing some planning together.

Sue Sum

As we agreed in our last faculty meeting, Bob, I've listed the key units I will cover this semester in the usual order.

Bob Beaker

Great, Sue! I made a similar list. Let's compare lists and see if there's a logical sequencing so that the units can have more match-up for students.

Sue Sum

Sounds good. It would be easy for me to adjust, and I like the idea of reinforcement of the concepts in math class.

Maria Novela

I've noticed you've listed your unit on pollution. I teach a similar literature unit on projecting future problems. Maybe we could plan some films or field experiences together.

Tom Time

You know, Maria, that makes a lot of sense. I'm glad we started looking at all of this. It's refreshing to juggle things around sometimes.

HOW TO INTEGRATE THE CURRICULA WORKING WITH MODEL 4: SEQUENCED

Essential Reasoning:

> "As ninth-grade teachers, we think it just makes sense to teach _____ in this department, while at the same time _____ teaches _____ in that class because one will enhance the other for the students."

Working with another teacher in another subject area, this template (Figure 4.4) is designed to help you see how changing the sequence of when certain units or topics are taught provides fertile ground for natural synchronization and integration. In essence, the process is simple: working with two different subject areas, the two teachers list their topics or units by the month on the lines at the bottom

Model 4: Sequenced

Social Studies	Language Arts
subject	subject

Sequence

Social Studies:
1. Medieval Times
2. American Revolution
3. Civil War
4. Women's Suffrage Movement
5. World War II
6. Depression
7. "Best Decade"
8. Region Report
9. Industrial Revolution
10. West

Language Arts:
1. *Robin Hood*
2. *The Midnight Ride of Paul Revere*
3. *The Slave Who Bought His Freedom*
4. *Nellie Bly*
5. *The Diary of Anne Frank*
6. Newspaper
7. Persuasive writing
8. Research Paper
9. Debate
10. Poetry

List

Social Studies:
1. Sept. – Amer. Hist. – Region Report
2. Oct. – Amer. Hist. – Civil War
3. Nov. – Amer. Hist. – Women's Suffrage
4. Dec. – World Hist. – Medieval Times
5. Jan. – World War II
6. Feb. – World Hist. – Region Report
7. Mar. – Amer. Hist. – Westward Movement
8. Apr. – Amer. Hist. – Industrial Revolution
9. May – Amer. Hist. – Decades
10. June – Amer. Hist. – Depression

Language Arts:
1. Sept. – *Robin Hood*
2. Oct. – *Nellie Bly*
3. Nov. – *Diary of Anne Frank*
4. Dec. – *The Midnight Ride of Paul Revere*
5. Jan. – *The Slave Who Bought His Freedom*
6. Feb. – Research Paper
7. Mar. – Persuasive Writing
8. Apr. – Debate
9. May – Poetry
10. June – Newspaper

Figure 4.1 Elementary School Example

Model 4: Sequenced

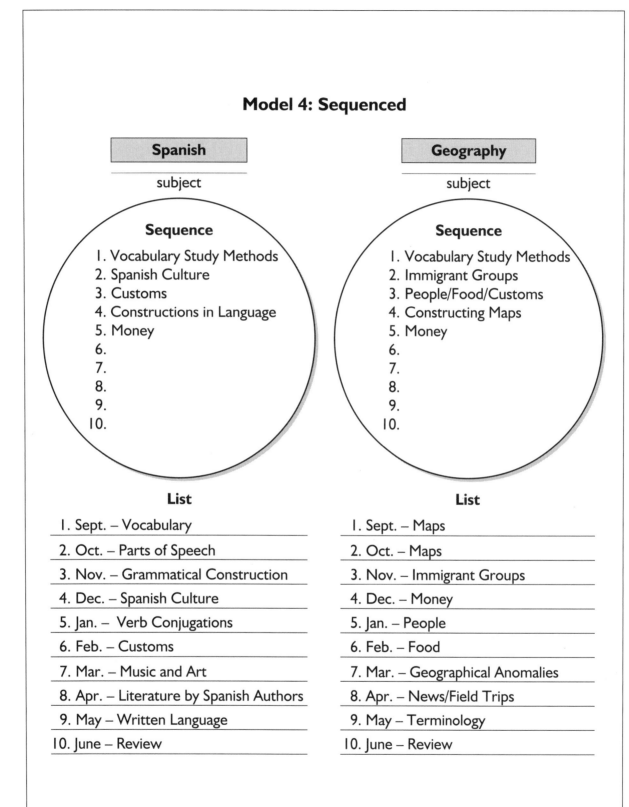

Spanish	Geography
subject	subject

Sequence

1. Vocabulary Study Methods
2. Spanish Culture
3. Customs
4. Constructions in Language
5. Money
6.
7.
8.
9.
10.

Sequence

1. Vocabulary Study Methods
2. Immigrant Groups
3. People/Food/Customs
4. Constructing Maps
5. Money
6.
7.
8.
9.
10.

List

1. Sept. – Vocabulary
2. Oct. – Parts of Speech
3. Nov. – Grammatical Construction
4. Dec. – Spanish Culture
5. Jan. – Verb Conjugations
6. Feb. – Customs
7. Mar. – Music and Art
8. Apr. – Literature by Spanish Authors
9. May – Written Language
10. June – Review

List

1. Sept. – Maps
2. Oct. – Maps
3. Nov. – Immigrant Groups
4. Dec. – Money
5. Jan. – People
6. Feb. – Food
7. Mar. – Geographical Anomalies
8. Apr. – News/Field Trips
9. May – Terminology
10. June – Review

Figure 4.2 Middle School Example

Model 4: Sequenced

Advanced Algebra	U.S. Geography
subject	subject

Sequence

1.
2.
3.
4.
5.
6.
7.
8.
9.
10.

No matches that made sense. Although no matches made sense, note the ideas in parentheses on the lists below. These are natural connections that occurred as the conversation proceeded. Each teacher can now talk with a more appropriate subject area teacher and try to sequence some things here.

Sequence

1.
2.
3.
4.
5.
6.
7.
8.
9.
10.

List

1. Sept. – Functions
2. Oct. – High-Degree Equations
3. Nov. – Conic Sections
4. Dec. – Logarithms (Chemistry?)
5. Jan. – Trig. Graphics (Physics?)

List

1. Sept. – U.S. Industry
2. Oct. – Growth of Factories
3. Nov. – Important U.S. Industries
4. Dec. – U.S. Industry Centers
5. Jan. – U.S. Business Centers (Careers?)

Figure 4.3   High School Example

of the page, giving a long look at the term. The listing represents the curricular scheme of things for the term or the year. It is the scope and sequence.

Then, after listing topics on the lines, the two teachers take turns talking about their sequence and why they teach certain things at various times. They try to find one or two parallel units to list in the circles above. There are often units that can be moved around to match up with each other's units; these are the parallel units that have potential for integration as the two teachers agree to teach the units at the same time.

The teachers do not team teach, but they do teach the targeted units simultaneously. They may share a film, a field trip, a speaker, but most things are done within their separate classrooms. The sequence is simply changed to provide a more connected approach for students. This is a simple model for two or three teachers to start integrating curricula.

Notes & Reflections
Model 4: Sequenced

Essential Reasoning:

"As ninth-grade teachers, we think it just makes sense to teach _____ in this department, while at the same time _____ teaches _____ in that class because one will enhance the other for the students."

Curriculum mapping is a foundational step toward curriculum integration. Simply mapping the curriculum, month by month or term by term, makes the scope and sequence of units visible and accessible to all teaches on a team or within a grade level.

The curriculum map can then be manipulated to maximize the natural connections between two units. Sequencing units with another teacher is an easy way to ensure that students see the connectivity between the skills and concepts that the two teachers are addressing in the process of teaching the units.

Finding opportunities to change the sequence of when something is taught is one of the easiest and earliest integration strategies to try. It does not require a great deal of team time once the sequence is established. Two teachers use a two step process: (1) list the traditional sequence of topics or units and (2) talk about which ones seem to go together, make a check mark by one or two of them.

More specifically, one partner lists the topics or units at the bottom of the graphic on the lines representing the various months and talks a little bit about the unit. Then the other partner does the same thing, listing and talking. Even as this is unfolding, the teachers will begin to see several ideas emerge that seem to go hand in hand. These are the units that they will both place in their respective circles at the top.

Now the teachers talk about these designated units to see whether they really can be switched around in terms of when the units occur during the term. Finally, they agree to try teaching them simultaneously in order to see if the obvious connections become more explicit for the students. If and when this occurs, students will have the advantage of reinforced concepts and skills as they attend both classes that are working on similar topics.

Again, with some basic curriculum mapping, the natural sequence of units often becomes quite noticeable as the map develops. This makes it easy to integrate across subjects simply by reorganizing two courses into parallel units.

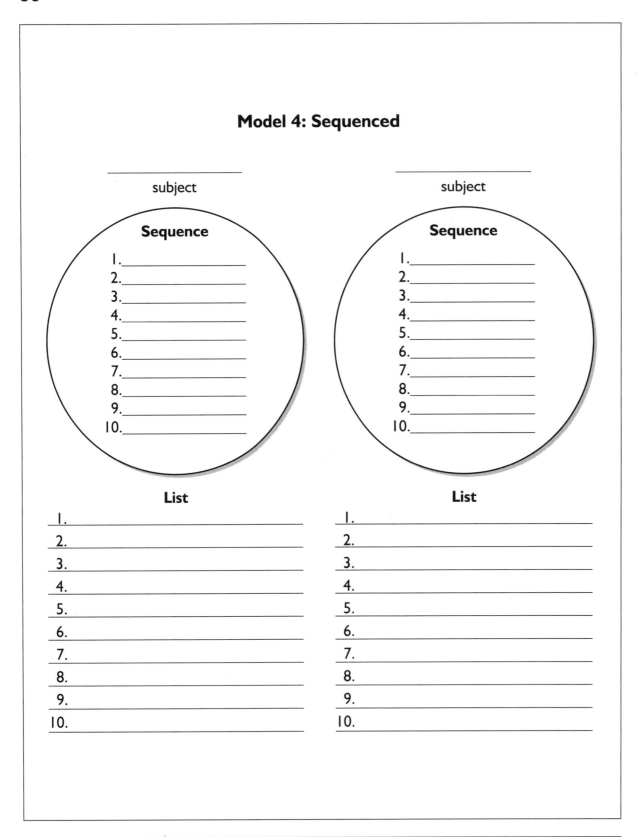

Model 4: Sequenced

subject _____

Sequence

1._____
2._____
3._____
4._____
5._____
6._____
7._____
8._____
9._____
10._____

subject _____

Sequence

1._____
2._____
3._____
4._____
5._____
6._____
7._____
8._____
9._____
10._____

List

1._____
2._____
3._____
4._____
5._____
6._____
7._____
8._____
9._____
10._____

List

1._____
2._____
3._____
4._____
5._____
6._____
7._____
8._____
9._____
10._____

Figure 4.4 On Your Own

Shared

*How are we collaborating
with other teachers to find the big
ideas that we share across disciplines?*

Binoculars—two disciplines that share overlapping concepts and skills	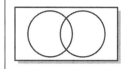 **Example** Science and mathematics teachers use data collection, charting, and graphing as shared concepts.

| Shared planning takes place in two disciplines in which overlapping concepts or ideas emerge as organizing elements. |

"The chief object of education is not to learn things, but to unlearn things."
—G. K. Chesterton

WHAT IS THE SHARED MODEL?

Certain broad disciplines create encompassing curricular umbrellas: mathematics and science paired as sciences; language arts and history coupled under the label of the humanities; art, music, dance, and drama viewed as the fine arts; and computer technology, industrial arts, and home arts embraced as the practical arts. Within these complementary disciplines, partner planning and teaching create a focus on shared concepts, skills, and attitudes that provide rich and robust integration of the curricula.

WHAT DOES IT LOOK LIKE?

In the shared model of curriculum integration, cross-departmental or cross–subject area teachers—whether at the elementary, middle, or high school level—partner to plan an in-depth unit of study. At least two members from two different disciplines approach the preliminary planning session with a notion of key concepts, skills, and attitudes that are traditionally taught within the single-subject approach. As the teachers identify their respective priorities, they look for overlaps in subject matter content by having real conversations about what they teach in a selected unit of study. For example, the literature teacher may focus on the concept of the American Dream as an organizer for a collection of short stories by American authors. At the same time, the history teacher notes that the unit on American history, which focuses on a study of each of the decades, could also use the American Dream as a unifying theme.

The shared model is based on shared ideas that come from within the disciplines. This model differs radically from the thematic approach in the conceptualization of unifying concepts because the concepts result from shared elements rather than the introduction of a theme from the outside. (The shared model is an inductive approach, emerging from various specific content, whereas the webbed or thematic model uses a deductive approach, with the shared concept identified and labeled prior to unit development.) This is what a Venn diagram (see Figures 5.1–5.4) represents—similarities in the overlapped section. The key is to look for concepts, topics, skills, attitudes, standards, and habits of mind that occur in both subjects.

To use the shared view of curricular integration, the teachers need to explore two disciplines for mutual concepts, skills, and attitudes as well as for actual content overlap. This process is more complex than simply sequencing a unit to coincide with one in another subject area. Rather than using a long look at the semester or year, teachers go in-depth with two units of study that are already designated for the current period of time.

WHAT DOES IT SOUND LIKE?

Elementary models of shared curricula embody standard planning models already in wide use. The self-contained classroom teacher plans the science unit on simple machines and the social studies unit on the Industrial Revolution around the concept of *efficiency*. This shared concept becomes the organizing umbrella. When using this model, teachers ask each other questions such as the following: What concepts do these units share? Are we teaching similar skills? Do the two units have shared ideas in terms of concepts, skills, attitudes, and standards?

WHAT ARE THE ADVANTAGES?

Advantages of this model of shared curriculum planning rest in its easy use as an early step toward more fully integrated models that encompass the four major disciplines. By coupling similar disciplines, the overlap facilitates deep learning of concepts for transfer. Simply put, it's easier to schedule common planning periods for a two-teacher team than it is to juggle the scheduling for a four-teacher team. In addition, planning often leads to shared instructional experiences, such as showing an appropriate film or planning a relevant field trip, because the two teachers may be able to put their two periods back to back in order to create a larger time block.

WHAT ARE THE DISADVANTAGES?

A barrier to shared curricula is the planning time needed to develop the units. In addition to time, flexibility and compromise are essential ingredients for successful implementation; it requires both trust and teamwork. This model of integration across two disciplines requires commitment from the partners to work through the initial phases. To find real overlap in curricular concepts requires in-depth dialogue and conversation.

WHEN IS THIS SHARED MODEL USEFUL?

This model is appropriate when subject areas are clustered into broad bands such as the humanities or practical arts. Also, this model facilitates early stages of implementation toward integrated curricula. It is a viable model to use with two disciplines as an intermediary step to teams of four disciplines that are much more complicated and complex. This model truly looks for those "roots running underground" because they bring cohesiveness to the curricula. It really searches for the conceptual understandings that are designated to be enduring—learning that follows students into real-world experiences.

Figures 5.1–5.3 are examples of completed shared model integration exercises, and Figure 5.4 provides the opportunity for readers to record their own design for this model.

Model 5:

Readers' Theater

"Try One!"

Narrator
Teachers at the school discuss possibilities for some shared curricular integration in the form of cross-departmental partnerships. Working in teams of two, they are discussing some planning ideas.

Sue Sum

I was intrigued by the number of students last semester who made explicit connections between what you were doing and what I was doing. The sequencing really seemed to foster the integration of the material.

Bob Beaker

You know, I had the same experience. They took much more notice of the similar contents than I expected. In fact, I never thought they'd notice at all.

Maria Novela

I suggested last year that we might share some films and field experiences. How would you feel about trying one short unit next semester, say, three weeks long?

Tom Time

I'm willing to try one if it is well planned and doesn't take too much time. Do you have one unit in particular in mind?

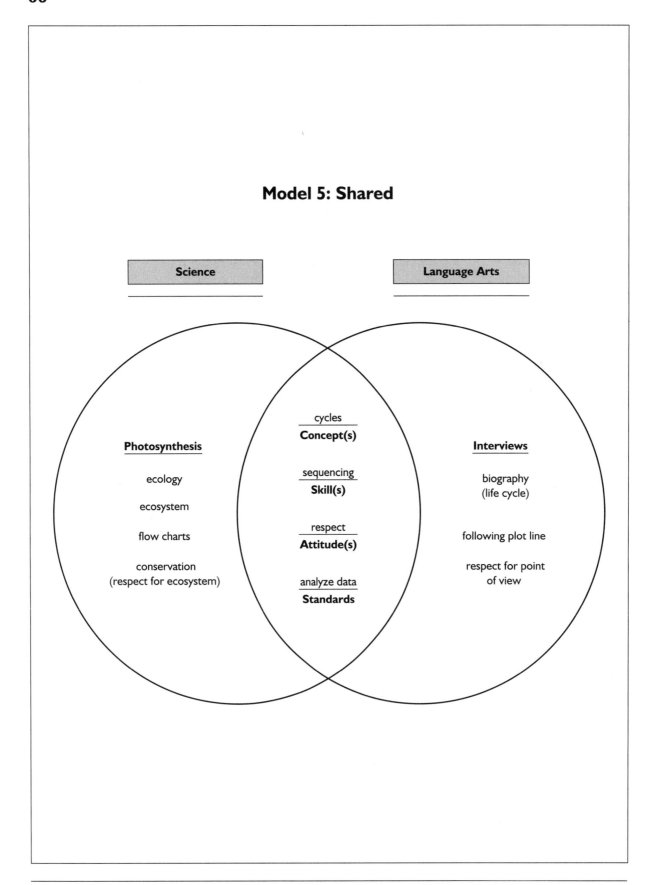

Figure 5.1   Elementary School Example

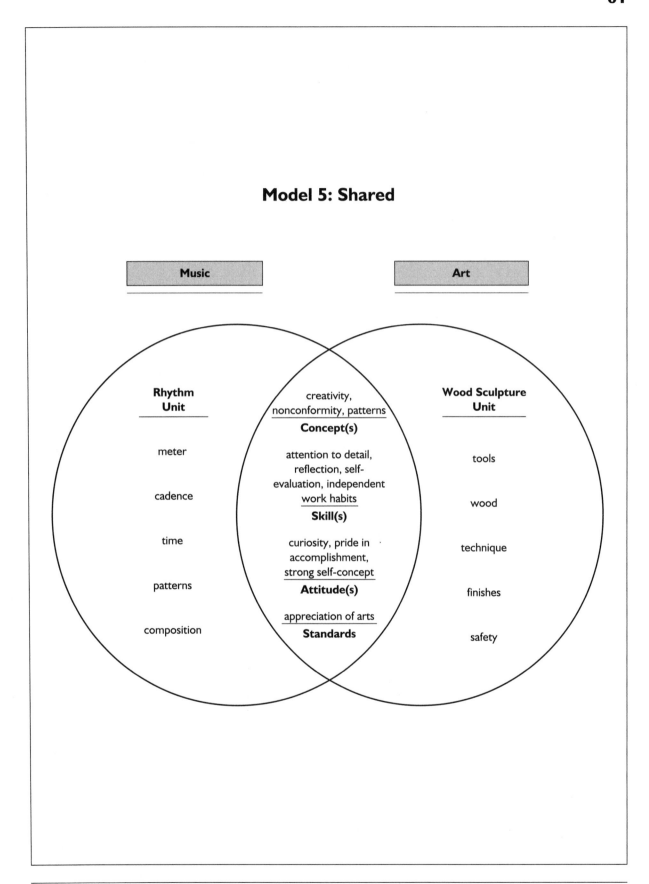

Model 5: Shared

Music	Art

Rhythm Unit

meter

cadence

time

patterns

composition

creativity, nonconformity, patterns
Concept(s)

attention to detail, reflection, self-evaluation, independent work habits
Skill(s)

curiosity, pride in accomplishment, strong self-concept
Attitude(s)

appreciation of arts
Standards

Wood Sculpture Unit

tools

wood

technique

finishes

safety

Figure 5.2   Middle School Example

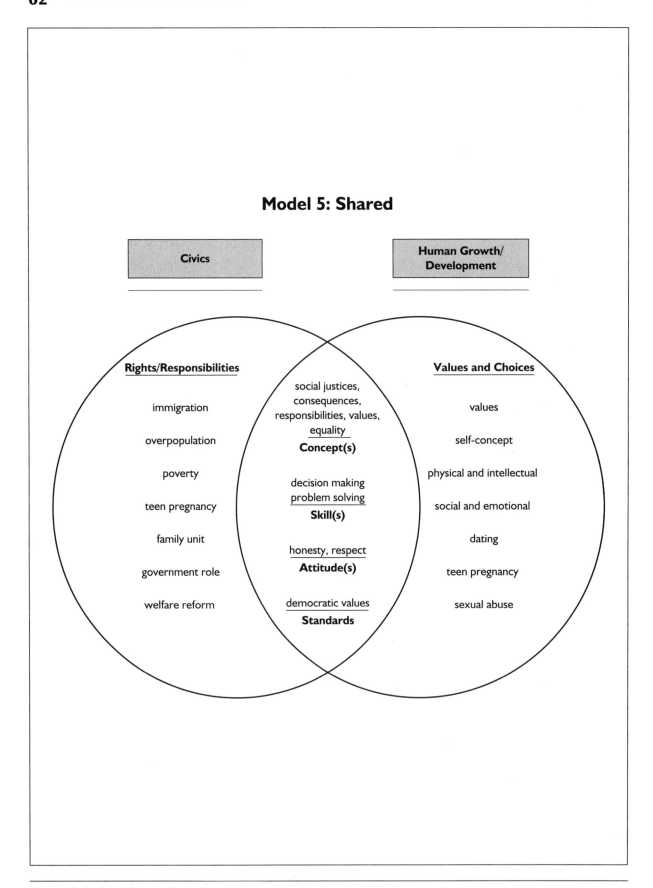

Figure 5.3   High School Example

HOW TO INTEGRATE THE CURRICULA WORKING WITH MODEL 5: SHARED

Essential Reasoning:

> *"We can dialogue in depth about a particular unit from our respective classes and find shared concepts, skills, and attitudes that seem to overlap."*

The template for this model (Figure 4.4) is designed for use with two different subject areas. It can be two teachers of the same grade level using two content areas or two teachers from different departments. The goal is to integrate curricula by looking in depth at the two units of study and finding the overlapping ideas, concepts, or skills.

Each of the partners thinks about particular units of study or standards-based topics that they teach. They decide on two units—one for each teacher—that seem to make a logical or commonsense match. (These may have been discovered in Model 4: Sequenced as teacher partners looked for ways to resequence their curricula.)

Using the Venn diagram in the template, the teachers take turns talking and writing in the outer circles about the units. Via in-depth conversation, they tell each other specifically what they do in the unit.

Then they find the concepts, skills, or attitudes (the content and the process standards) that the two units share and overlapping ideas that the units have in common. The teachers use the most robust idea to create a thematic focus around a key concept or a skill focus that duplicates practice with life skills addressed in both units.

Notes & Reflections
Model 5: Shared

Essential Reasoning:

> *"We can dialogue in depth about a particular unit from our respective classes, and find shared concepts, skills and attitudes that seem to overlap."*

It's true that topics and units from two related or unrelated disciplines can offer rich possibilities for integration. Identifying basic concepts, skills, attitudes, and standards that overlap enables the commonalities among these distinct disciplines to readily emerge.

It really is such a surprise to see how much the two disciplines have in common as teachers share the details of their units with each other. They may have thought that their disciplines were so far apart and so separate.

It can be very energizing to see so many shared ideas and to think about how these will be addressed fully in both classrooms and what a boost the collaboration will provide for the kids. Benefits abound with this collaborative approach.

"We can't wait to get started and to try this with other units. This curriculum integration planning model is at the top of our list because we only need to have time to meet with one other teacher, rather than with a whole team. Also, we are thinking about what other teachers and disciplines we might meet with to talk about our units. We believe that this is a viable model that could be used many times over."

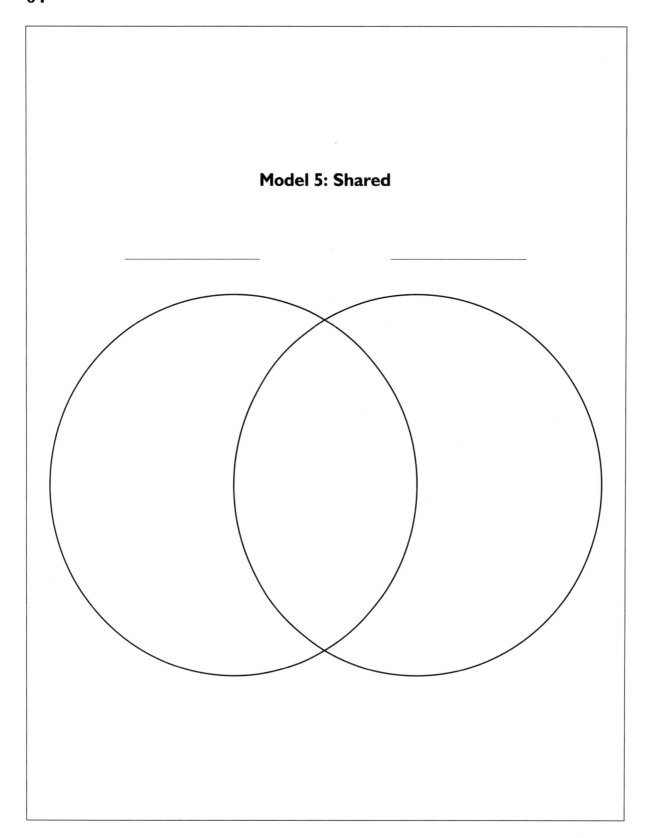

Model 5: Shared

Figure 5.4   On Your Own

Are we or how are we using patterns and themes to integrate the curricula?

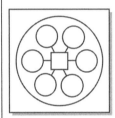

Webbed curricula represent the thematic approach to integrating subject matter.

Telescope—broad view of an entire constellation as one theme, webbed to the various elements.

Example

The teacher presents a simple topical theme, such as the circus, and webs it to the subject areas. A conceptual theme, such as conflict, can be webbed for a broader reach in the theme approach.

"We must open the doors of opportunity. But we must also equip our people to walk through those doors."

—Lyndon B. Johnson

WHAT IS THE WEBBED MODEL?

Webbed curricula represent the thematic approach to integrating subject matter. Typically, this thematic approach to curriculum development begins with a theme such as transportation or inventions. After a cross-departmental team has decided on a theme, it uses the theme as an overlay to the different subjects: *inventions* lead to the study of simple machines in science, reading and writing about inventors in language arts, designing and building models in industrial arts, drawing and studying Rube Goldberg contraptions in mathematics, and making flowcharts in computer technology classes. In more sophisticated webbed models, intricate units of study can be developed in which integration occurs in all relevant curricular areas to cluster and address standards through robust curriculum models.

WHAT DOES IT LOOK LIKE?

In departmentalized situations, the webbed curricular approach to integration is often achieved through the use of a fairly generic but fertile theme such as patterns or cycles. This conceptual theme provides rich possibilities for the inherent diversities of various disciplines. And it has more reach across disciplines; it is more generalizable.

While similar conceptual themes, such as structures or conflict, provide fertile ground for cross-disciplinary units of study, elementary models can also use a book or a genre of books as the topic to thematically organize their curricula. For example, fairy tales or dog stories can become catalysts for curricular webbing. Typical lists look like Figure 6.1.

WHAT DOES IT SOUND LIKE?

When searching for a theme, teacher teams generally begin with an idea-gathering session that involves a lot of genuine interaction, conversation, and dialogue among colleagues: "How about this one?" "What do you think of this?" "I read about a school that used cultural diversity as an overriding theme." "Let's brainstorm a long list. I don't want to use the first one we think of just to be done with it." "Maybe we should ask the students for their ideas." "I have some lists of theme ideas from a workshop." "Yeah, but we will need to look at that list carefully and compare them to some criteria. I have Perkin's criteria here." And so it goes as they explore possibilities and set guidelines for reaching a decision. Figure 6.2 provides criteria for selecting possible themes.

In selecting a theme, it is important to generate lots of questions. It helps to explore the depth and breadth of a theme, which often leads to a kid-friendly tagline (e.g., Change: What Goes Around, Comes Around; Change: The End Is The Beginning).

Concepts	Topics	Problems
• freedom	• space	• hostages
• cooperation	• birds	• recycling
• challenge	• reactions	• school funding
• conflict	• the world	• revolution
• discovery	• World War I	• drought/flood
• culture	• rainforest	• cultural clash
• change	• partnerships	• pollution
• argument and evidence	• kites	• energy crisis
• perseverance	• bridges	• war
	• light	• global warming

Figure 6.1   A Look at Webbed Models

A good lens . . . applies BROADLY
A good lens . . . applies PERVASIVELY
A good lens . . . discloses FUNDAMENTAL PATTERNS
A good lens . . . reveals SIMILARITIES and CONTRASTS
A good lens . . . FASCINATES

Figure 6.2   Fertile Themes for Integrative Learning Are Like a Good Lens

SOURCE: From "Selecting Fertile Themes for Integrated Learning," by D. N. Perkins, in H. H. Jacobs (Ed.), *Interdisciplinary Curriculum: Design and Implementation* (pp. 67–76), 1989, Alexandria, VA: Association for Supervision and Curriculum Development.

WHAT ARE THE ADVANTAGES?

An advantage of the webbed approach to curricular integration is the motivational factor that results from selecting high-interest themes. In addition, the webbed model or unit-writing approach is familiar to seasoned teachers and is a fairly straightforward curriculum planning model for less experienced teachers to grasp. Thematic units are multidisciplinary units that make it easy to address various content standards yet keep an overall focus or pattern. The webbed model also facilitates teamwork planning as cross-departmental teams work to weave a theme into all content areas. This model provides a visible and motivational umbrella for students; it is easy for them to see how different activities and ideas are connected. It is often easy to brainstorm different activities, projects, and products that mirror the selected themes. In fact, it is through the creative process of thematic development that teachers and students become energized with the many possibilities.

WHAT ARE THE DISADVANTAGES?

The most serious difficulty with the webbed model lies in the selection of a theme. There is a tendency to grab at shallow themes that are superficially useful in curriculum planning. Often these artificial themes lead to a contrived curriculum. Also, caution must be taken not to sacrifice the logical and necessary scope and sequence inherent in the disciplines. In this model, teachers can get bogged down in curriculum writing that may not warrant the time involved as compared to long-term use of the thematic unit in years to come. Yet if a theme is used from year to year, so that over time a number of thematic units have been developed and "banked" for recycling, the time is worth it. Another disadvantage of this model is that teachers can become focused on activities rather than on concept development, so caution should be taken to keep the content relevant and rigorous.

WHEN IS THIS WEBBED MODEL USEFUL?

Although themes are used by one teacher in a single classroom, the webbed model for integrating curriculum is often a team approach that takes time to develop. Summer curriculum writing time is an opportune period to initiate this model so that teachers can fully explore theme options and set criteria for quality. This model often takes planning and coordination among various departments and special subject areas. It is a great model to use when trying a two- to four-week interdisciplinary pilot unit. Because of the planning needed to execute this model well, it is advisable to start with a manageable piece of the curriculum.

Instead of webbing a theme to the various disciplines, try webbing it to multiple intelligences (Gardner 1983, 1999). Figure 6.3 shows the eight intelligences and activities that relate to each. Develop a grid with eight columns and try to place activities for the different intelligences for each cell in the grid.

Figure 6.4 shows a grid with the eight intelligences and ideas for types of activities. Figure 6.5 is a grid for teachers to use in identifying specific readings or activities for each intelligence as an integrated unit is developed around

Multiple Ways to Experience Learning

Verbal-Linguistic	Visual-Spatial	Logical-Mathematical	Musical-Rhythmic	Interpersonal-Social	Intrapersonal-Introspective	Bodily-Kinesthetic	Naturalist-Physical World
reporting	storyboarding	reasoning	singing	discussing	journaling	dancing	observing
writing essays	painting	collecting	listening	responding	feeling	sculpting	discovering
creating stories	cartooning	recording	playing	dialoging	reflecting	performing	uncovering
reciting	observing	analyzing	composing	interviewing	logging	preparing	observing
listing	drawing	graphing	audiotapes	surveying	meditating	constructing	digging
telling/retelling	illustrating	comparing/contrasting	improvising	questioning	studying	acting	planting
listening	diagramming	classifying	recording	paraphrasing	rehearsing	role-playing	comparing
labeling	depicting	ranking	selecting music	clarifying	self-assessing	dramatizing	displaying
dialoging	showing	evaluating	critiquing music	affirming	remembering	pantomiming	sorting

Figure 6.3   Multiple Intelligences Grid of Ideas

Multiple Types of Activities

Verbal-Linguistic	Visual-Spatial	Logical-Mathematical	Musical-Rhythmic	Interpersonal-Social	Intrapersonal-Introspective	Bodily-Kinesthetic	Naturalist-Physical World
printouts	mosaics	mazes	performance	group projects	journals	role-playing	field trips
debates	paintings	puzzles	songs	group tasks	meditations	dramatizing	field studies
poetry	drawings	outlines	musicals	observation	self-assessments	skits	bird watching
jokes	sketches	matrices	instruments	charts	intuiting	body language	observing nests
speeches	illustrations	sequences	rhythms	social	logs	facial	planting
reading	cartoons	patterns	compositions	interactions	records	expressions	photographing
storytelling	sculptures	logic	harmonies	dialogues	reflections	dancing	nature walks
listening	models	analogies	chords	conversations	quotations	gestures	forecasting
audiotapes	constructions	time lines	trios/duos	debates	"I" statements	pantomiming	weather
essays	maps	equations	quartets	arguments	creative	field trips	star gazing
reports	storyboards	formulas	beat	consensus	expression	lab work	fishing
crosswords	videotapes	theorems	melodies	communication	goals	interviews	exploring caves
fiction	photographs	calculations	raps	collages	affirmations	sports	categorizing
nonfiction	symbols	computations	jingles	murals	insight	games	rocks
newspapers	visual aids	syllogisms	choral	mosaics	poetry	manipulatives	ecology studies
magazines	posters	codes	readings	round robins	interpretations	investigations	catching
Internet research	murals	games	scores	sports	writing	walkabout	butterflies
books	doodles	probabilities	choirs	games	sketching	explorations	shell collecting
biographies	statues	fractions	chorus	challenges	doodling	hands-on	identifying
bibliographies	collages	problem solving	listening	teamwork	wondering	learning	plants
research	mobiles	measurement	recording		musing	simulations	
	graphics	metric					
	comics						
	ads						

Figure 6.4   Multiple Intelligences Grid of Activities

Unit: _____

In each column, list specific activities for that intelligence which relate to the overall topic or concept targeted in the theme.

Verbal-Linguistic	Visual-Spatial	Interpersonal-Social	Intrapersonal-Introspective	Mathematical-Logical	Musical-Rhythmic	Naturalist-Physical World	Bodily-Kinesthetic

Figure 6.5 Blank Multiple Intelligences Grid

multiple intelligences. It is a variation of the webbed model that targets differentiated learning through multiple intelligences.

Figures 6.6–6.8 are examples of completed webbed model integration exercises, and Figure 6.9 provides the opportunity for readers to record their own design for this model.

Model 6: Webbed
Readers' Theater

"Oh, the Webs We Weave"

Narrator

At the staff meeting, our teachers commit to do a three-week theme.

Maria Novela

I am excited about selecting a theme that can be webbed to all the contents. It takes me back to my college days when we used to write interdisciplinary units. The pendulum does swing, doesn't it?

Tom Time

You know, I had the same thought. I think this design is worthwhile. It will pull what were separate and disparate parts of the curriculum together for the kids.

Maria Novela

Yes! Remember the article we read on finding fertile themes? The criteria set forth by Perkins in that piece seemed quite useful. Do you remember what they were?

Sue Sum

I have the article right here. Let's brainstorm some ideas and selectively abandon the more superficial ones. I have too many priorities to waste time. I want activities to be meaningful.

Bob Beaker

It looks like we have two categories: topical themes and conceptual themes. Let's sort that out first. Then we can compare the theme to the criteria from the Perkins article that Tom just listed on the chalkboard.

Model 6: Webbed

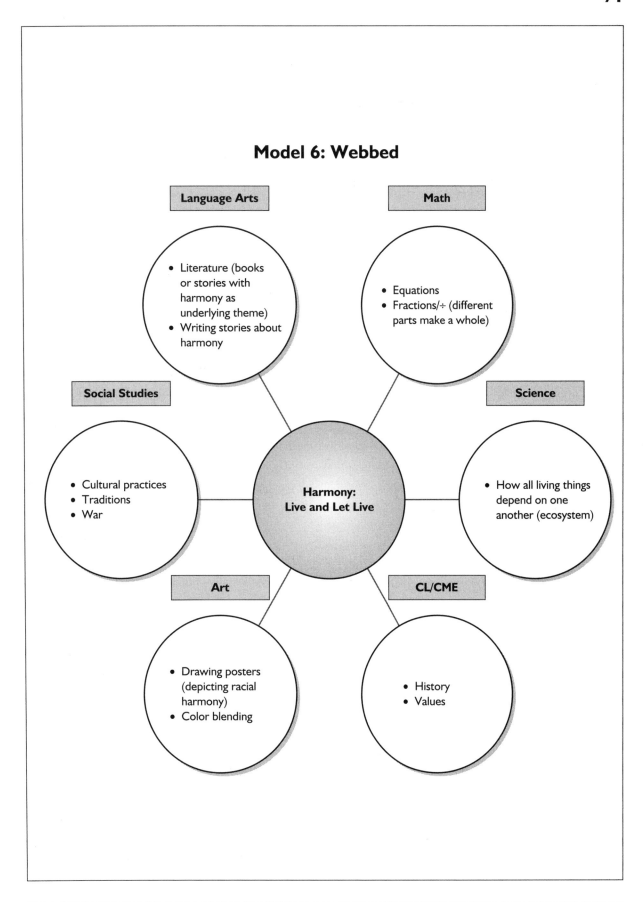

Language Arts
- Literature (books or stories with harmony as underlying theme)
- Writing stories about harmony

Math
- Equations
- Fractions/÷ (different parts make a whole)

Social Studies
- Cultural practices
- Traditions
- War

Harmony: Live and Let Live

Science
- How all living things depend on one another (ecosystem)

Art
- Drawing posters (depicting racial harmony)
- Color blending

CL/CME
- History
- Values

HOT Questions: Harmony

1. What is the role of harmony in math?

2. What is the impact of harmony?

3. Why is harmony important?

4. How can we create harmony?

5. Does harmony help us achieve our goals?

6. Does harmony impact everyone?

7. What is harmony?

8. How do we teach harmony?

9. How do we maintain harmony?

10. How do we assess pupils' understanding of harmony?

11. When do you feel disharmony?

12. Is harmony good?

13. How is harmony hurtful?

14. Why is harmony harmonious?

15. Is harmony only in music?

16. Can I affect harmony?

17. Does harmony impact everyone?

18. Is harmony desirable at any cost?

19. What is the cost of harmony in a relationship?

20. Can harmony rule supreme?

Figure 6.6 Elementary School Example

Model 6: Webbed

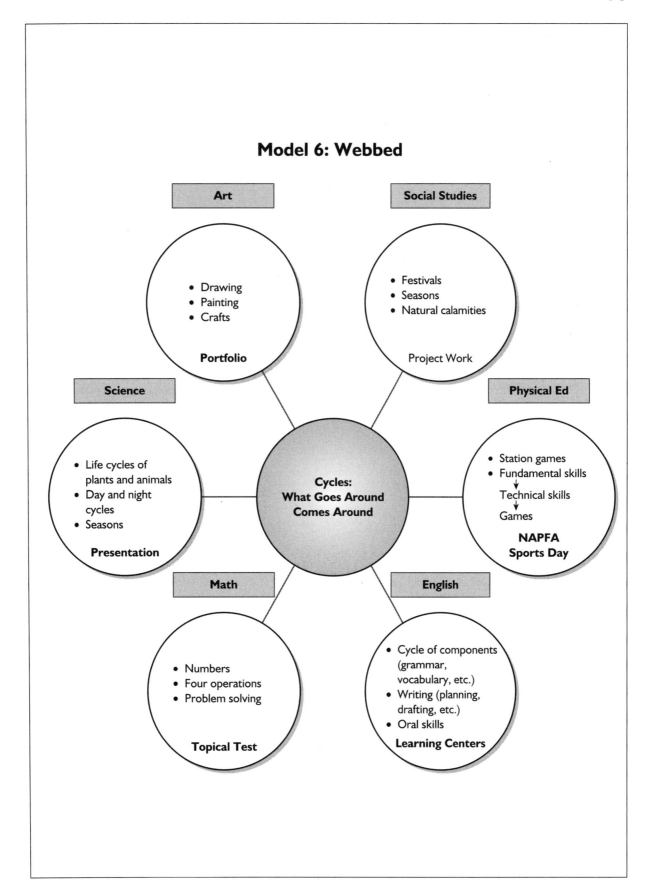

HOT Questions: Cycles

1. How powerful are cycles?

2. How do they affect us?

3. Why are cycles important?

4. Why do they exist?

5. What would happen if there were a disruption in a cycle?

6. How do cycles relate to changes in the world?

7. What problems do they pose to the world?

8. When is the end the beginning?

9. When is the beginning the end?

10. How do you break a cycle?

11. Is a cycle continuous?

12. Why recycle?

13. How does a cycle look? Feel?

14. When is a cycle cyclical?

15. Am I cycling around?

16. What kinds of cycles are there?

17. How is cycling like a _____?

18. Is there a cycle of life? History? Politics? Economics? Weather?

19. Cycle this!

20. Recycle that!

Figure 6.7   Middle School Example

Model 6: Webbed

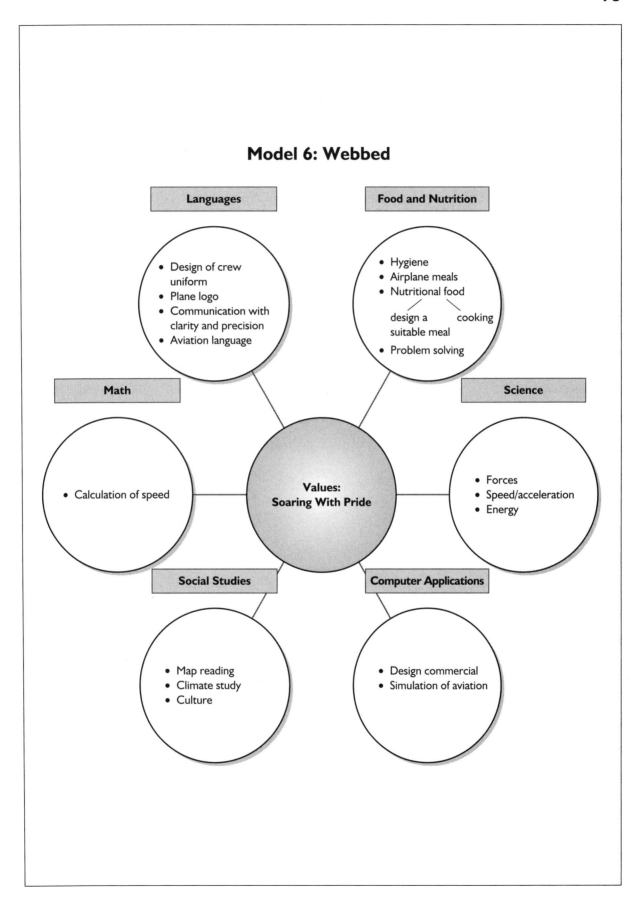

HOT Questions: Values

1. What are values?

2. How are values important?

3. What do people value?

4. What are the school values?

5. What do the students/parents value?

6. What do I value?

7. What values does aeromodeling present?

8. Science values?

9. Language values?

10. Are social values reliable?

11. What are values on the Internet?

12. What is the role of values in math and science?

13. Are values valued?

14. How are values valued?

15. Do you value what I value?

16. Should we value the same thing?

17. What is devaluing the dollar?

18. How does someone devalue you?

19. Where do you keep your valuables?

20. Are valuables the same as values?

Figure 6.8 High School Example

HOW TO INTEGRATE THE CURRICULA
WORKING WITH MODEL 6: WEBBED

Essential Reasoning:

> *"We like to organize the various subject-oriented standards of our grade level or department around a big-idea thematic unit so that students learn the curriculum in a more coherent manner."*

Using a list of themes generated by a grade-level or department team, select one that seems to meet the criteria for fertile themes: applies broadly and pervasively, discloses fundamental patterns, reveals similarities and differences, and fascinates both students and teachers.

Once the theme is selected, add a kid-friendly tagline to give it more focus. The tagline expresses the essence of the theme for students. Here are a few examples:

Fashion: Whose Statement Is It?
Energy: Vroooooom!
Astronomy: The Stars Are Out

Work around the web (Figure 6.9), labeling the various disciplines represented by the grade-level subject matter or the content from various departments. Then proceed to insert learning experiences for the subject or departments represented.

Complete the discussion by adding spokes to each subject area to indicate the targeted standards and assessments.

Notes & Reflections
Model 6: Webbed

Essential Reasoning:

> *"We like to organize the various subject-oriented standards of our grade level or department around a big-idea thematic unit so that students learn the curriculum in a more coherent manner."*

In this webbed model, the selection of a theme provides a fresh lens with which to frame and view various subject matter content. The theme acts as a giant umbrella that is visible and real to students as they work in the various content areas.

In selecting the theme, teachers can find the big ideas that are inherent in the curriculum. And as they brainstorm all the possible themes, they can also see the kinds of concepts, topics, or problems that tend to emerge in their discussions. That, in turn, gives teachers the opportunity to group the themes into various categories in a coding process. This can be a helpful way to examine the content of the curriculum at each grade level.

Going on to select the best theme from the collection of ideas, teachers truly explore the richness of each theme and its potential for addressing major learning standards. They have a chance to look for the theme's breadth and depth as well as interest and intrigue.

Finally, while inserting activities, teachers have a chance to indicate the various standards addressed as well as the possible or likely assessment strategies. In brief, the theme provides a way to look at the various standards (the spokes emanating from the circles) that are addressed in a robust, thematic unit.

This is not only an easy integration model for learners but also an energizing one for teachers.

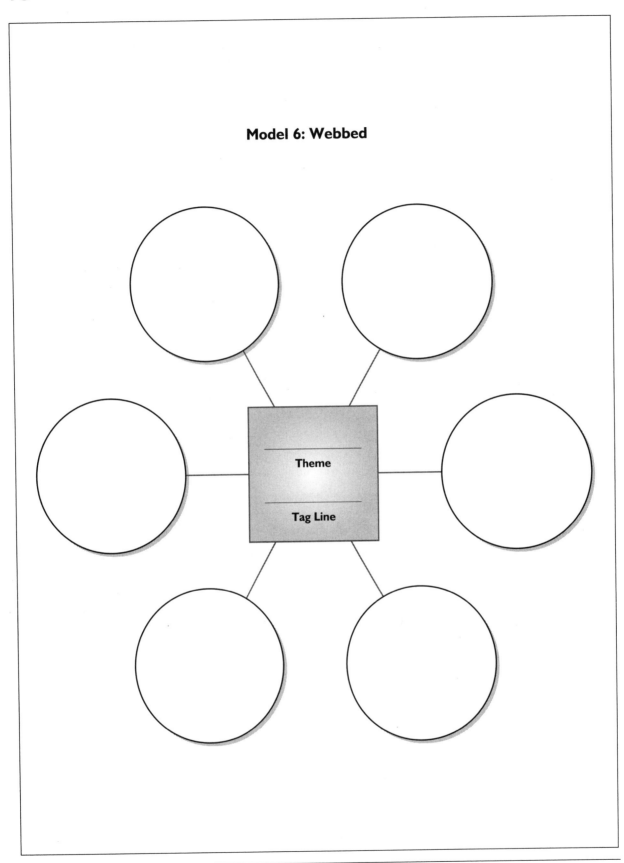

Model 6: Webbed

Theme

Tag Line

Figure 6.9 On Your Own

Threaded

*Are we or how are we threading
skills across the various content areas?*

Magnifying glass—life skills that magnify all
content through a metacurricular approach

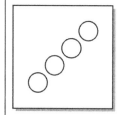

Example

The teaching staff targets prediction in reading,
mathematics, and science lab experiments
while the social studies teacher targets
predicting current events, and thus threads
prediction across all four disciplines.

Standards, thinking
skills, social skills,
study skills, graphic
organizers, technology,
and a multiple
intelligences approach
to learning thread
through all disciplines.

*"The great end of an education is to discipline rather than to furnish the mind.
To train it to the use of its own powers rather than to fill it with the accumulation of others."*
—Tryon Edwards

WHAT IS THE THREADED MODEL?

This threaded model of curricular integration focuses on the metacurriculum
that supersedes or intersects the very heart of any and all subject matter content. For example, prediction is a skill used to estimate in math, forecast in current events, anticipate events in a story in English, and hypothesize in the
science lab. Consensus-seeking strategies are used to resolve conflicts in any
problem-solving situation. These skills are, in essence, threaded through standard curricular content. They are life skills that can be successfully targeted
with various content.

WHAT DOES IT LOOK LIKE?

The threaded model looks like the now commonly accepted models of writing across the content areas, reading across the content areas. or even technology integration. Using the idea of a metacurriculum, or curricular concerns that go beyond the actual content concerns, grade-level or departmental teams might target a set of thinking skills to infuse into existing content priorities. For example, using the thinking skills chart in Figure 7.1, *compare and contrast* might be the thinking skill that the freshmen team chooses to thread across content. Likewise, one of the multiple intelligences (Figure 7.2), a social skill (Figure 7.3), a study skill, a standard (Figure 7.4), a graphic organizer, or a performance could be threaded through various disciplines.

WHAT DOES IT SOUND LIKE?

As the standards, thinking skills, social skills, graphic organizers, or multiple intelligences are threaded into the content, teachers ask appropriate

---

Balancing your choices with skills from critical thinking clusters and creative thinking clusters, select microskills to thread through the curriculum for a period of time. By changing the skill each month or so, you reinforce various thinking habits for students as the skills are threaded into the class work throughout the school. Students encounter the skills in different contexts.

Critical Thinking Skills	Macroprocesses	Creative Thinking Skills
Attribute Cluster	Problem solving	*Perception Cluster*
Classify	Decision making	Predict
Compare and contrast	Creative ideation	Image
Sequence		Invent
Prioritize	**Graphic Organizers**	Hypothesize
Solve analogies	Web	Visualize
	Map	Discern patterns
Analysis Cluster	Flowchart	
Analyze for bias	Venn	*Inference Cluster*
Analyze for assumptions	Matrix	Predict
Draw conclusions	Fishbone	Infer
	KWL	Imply
Evaluation Cluster	PMI	Generalize
Evaluate	Thought tree	Hypothesize
Solve analogies	Chain of events	
Analyze for assumptions		*Brainstorm Cluster*
Analyze for bias		Personify
Critique		Brainstorm
		Invent
Sequence Cluster		Visualize
Sequence		Associate
Prioritize		Discern patterns
Discern cause and effect		
Draw conclusions		

Figure 7.1 Examples of Thinking Skills as Threads

Using Gardner's (1983, 1999) theory of multiple intelligences, select from the eight identified intelligences and thread one through the content for a period of time. (Some schools thread a different intelligence each month as a way to familiarize teachers, students, and parents with the theory of multiple intelligences.) Looking at prodigies in a particular field helps illustrate the various dimensions of each intelligence.

Verbal-Linguistic: abilities in reading, writing, speaking, and listening

> Prodigies: writing—Maya Angelou; speaking—Martin Luther King; reading—Abraham Lincoln; listening—Johnny Carson

Visual-Spatial: abilities in the visual arts, architecture, and design

> Prodigies: painting—Claude Monet; sculpture—Auguste Rodin; architecture—Frank Lloyd Wright; design—Jackson Pollock

Mathematical-Logical: abilities in mathematical ideas, logic, and reasoning

> Prodigies: mathematics—Sir Isaac Newton; logic—Albert Einstein; reasoning—Aristotle

Musical-Rhythmic: abilities to appreciate, compose, and perform musically

> Prodigies: appreciation—Leonard Bernstein; composing—Wolfgang Amadeus Mozart; performing—Itzak Perlman

Interpersonal-Social: abilities with interpersonal relationships in the social realm

> Prodigies: interpersonal skills—John F. Kennedy; relationships—Dale Carnegie; social realm—Florence Nightingale

Intrapersonal-Introspective: abilities to understand the inner world of the self, to understand intrinsic motivations, and to know oneself

> Prodigies: inner world—Mahatma Gandhi; intrinsic motivation—Bertrand Russell; knowledge of self—Socrates

Bodily-Kinesthetic: abilities to develop body awareness, to manipulate the muscles, and to develop motor agility

> Prodigies: develop body awareness—Michael Jordan; manipulate the muscles—Margot Fonteyn; develop motor agility—Tiger Woods

Naturalist-Physical World: abilities to understand, relate to, and classify the natural world

> Prodigies: animal species—Charles Darwin; birds—James Audubon; sea—Jacques Cousteau; planetary universe—Carl Sagan

Figure 7.2 Examples of Multiple Intelligences as Threads

Select appropriate social skills to thread through various classes. Choose from the four major categories of social skills: communication, team building/trust, leadership, and conflict resolution. By varying the category, you expose students to a number of social skills over time.

Communication	Team Building/Trust	Leadership	Conflict Resolution
• Use six-inch voice • Listen to others • Clarify • Paraphrase • Give examples • Sense tone • Associate ideas • Extend ideas • Affirm others	• Keep an open mind • Respect each other's opinion • Accept each other's ideas • Listen with focus • Build on each other's ideas	• Help each other • Take responsibility • Accept a group role • Contribute ideas • Let all participate • Encourage others • Include all members • Synthesize ideas	• Disagree with the idea, not the person • Seek consensus • Generate alternatives • Reach consensus • Justify ideas • Learn how to agree to disagree

Figure 7.3 Examples of Social Skills as Threads

Students will acquire knowledge and skills to

- identify problems and their elements
- speak and write standard English
- justify sound decisions
- understand democratic principles
- perform and produce works of art
- compute numerical functions
- organize data into useful forms
- use the principles of movement
- discover and evaluate patterns

Figure 7.4   Generic Standards of Learning as Threads

questions such as "How did you think about that?," "What thinking skill did you find most helpful?," "How well did your group work today?," and "Have you used your musical intelligences today?" These processing questions contrast sharply with the usual cognitive questions such as "What answer did you get?" and "How many of you agree?" (Sometimes, the metacognitive questions sound to students like the teacher is off track. Students will often say, "OK, what are we supposed to do?" to try to get back to the task at hand.)

WHAT ARE THE ADVANTAGES?

Advantages of the threaded model revolve around the concept of the meta-curriculum: the awareness and control of the skills and strategies of thinking and learning that go beyond the subject matter content. Teachers stress the metacognitive behavior so that students learn about *how* they are learning. By making students aware of the learning processes, teachers facilitate future transfer. Not only does the content stay pure for each discipline, but also the students reap the added benefit of an extraordinary kind of thinking that can transfer into life skills. In addition, each of the disciplines is enhanced by supporting the life skills.

WHAT ARE THE DISADVANTAGES?

A disadvantage of the threaded model is the necessity of adding "another" curriculum, such as a thinking or social skills curriculum. Content connections across subject areas are not addressed explicitly. The metacurriculum surfaces, but the disciplines remain static. Connections between and among the content matter of the subjects are not necessarily stressed. Also, to thread the metacurriculum through the content, all teachers need an understanding of those skills and strategies. But developing a list of the skills teachers address often leads to a rich and meaningful discussion about various life skills.

WHEN IS THIS THREADED MODEL USEFUL?

This model is useful in integrating curricula when a metacurriculum of thinking and social skills is a district focus. This model is appropriate to use as one of the alternative steps toward intense subject matter integration. The threaded model also is easier to sell to hardcore curriculum advocates who are reluctant to shift subject matter priorities. Therefore, this becomes a viable high school model to start with as teachers keep their content intact and infuse thinking, cooperating, and multiple intelligences into that content.

Figures 7.5–7.10 are examples of completed threaded model integration exercises, and Figure 7.11 provides the opportunity for readers to record their own design for this model.

Model 7 Threaded

Readers' Theater

"A Little Dab Will Do Ya!"

Narrator

Our teachers find it easy to thread certain skills, such as inferring, through their particular contents.

Bob Beaker

So, our teacher terms will focus on the thinking skill of inferring. The science classes will target inference and observation as key skills.

Tom Time

Right, Bob, inferring from data and predicting trends, both in a historical sense and in future studies, also has potential to enrich the curriculum content. At first, I was afraid the subject matter would lose and we would dilute the disciplines, but this actually is enhancing my content!

Maria Novela

Reading between the lines, making inferences, is an absolute basic expectation of good readers. I think the study of literature this semester will be expected to go beyond the literal information presented.

Sue Sum

And inferring from graphs, charts, and data is a natural for math class. With the overload of information and the increased use of graphics, students need work in making inferences from the gathered data. It's a rich thread to string through contents.

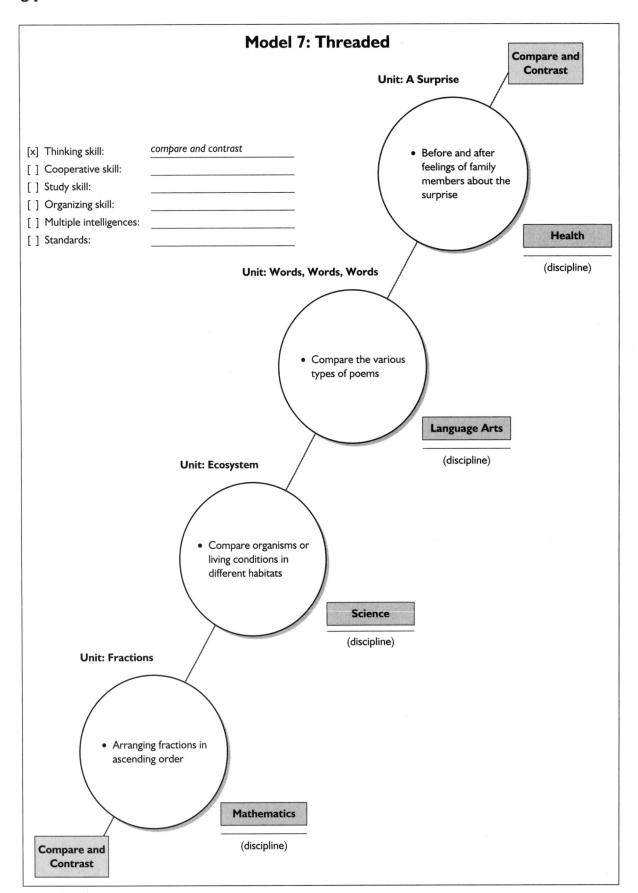

Figure 7.5 Elementary School Example

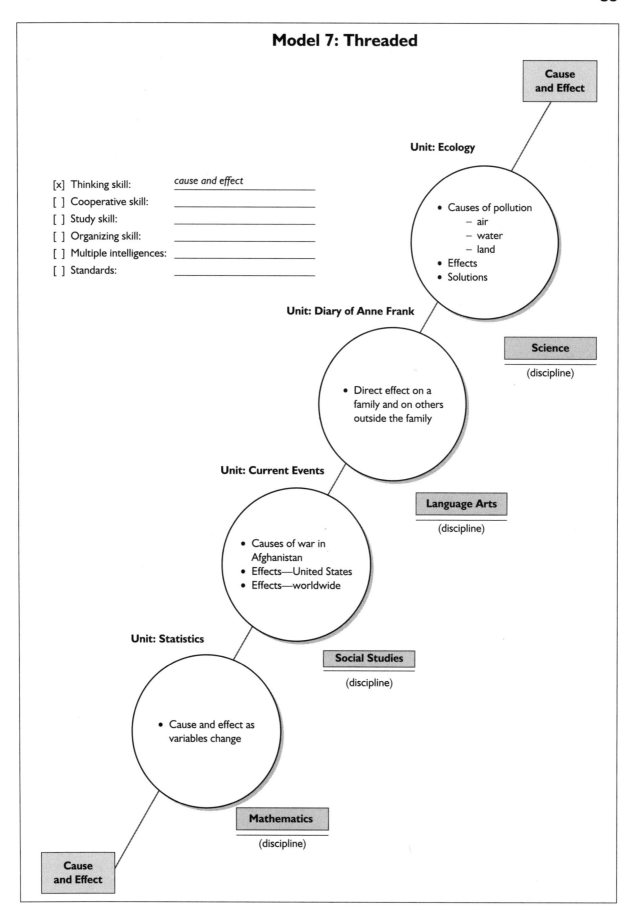

Figure 7.6   Middle School Example

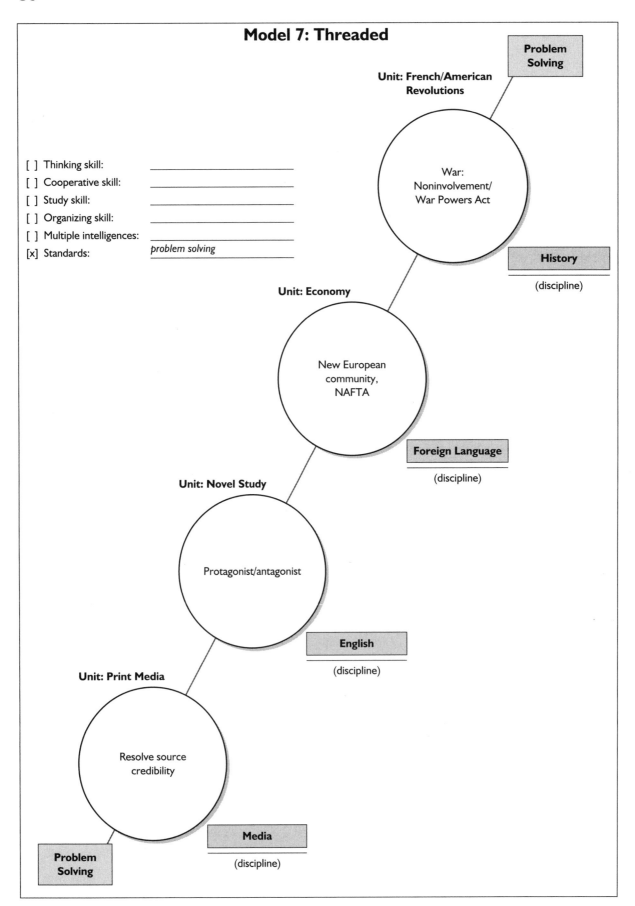

Model 7: Threaded

Unit: French/American Revolutions

War: Noninvolvement/ War Powers Act

Problem Solving

History
(discipline)

Unit: Economy

New European community, NAFTA

Foreign Language
(discipline)

Unit: Novel Study

Protagonist/antagonist

English
(discipline)

Unit: Print Media

Resolve source credibility

Media
(discipline)

Problem Solving

[ ] Thinking skill: _____
[ ] Cooperative skill: _____
[ ] Study skill: _____
[ ] Organizing skill: _____
[ ] Multiple intelligences: _____
[x] Standards: *problem solving* _____

Figure 7.7 High School Example

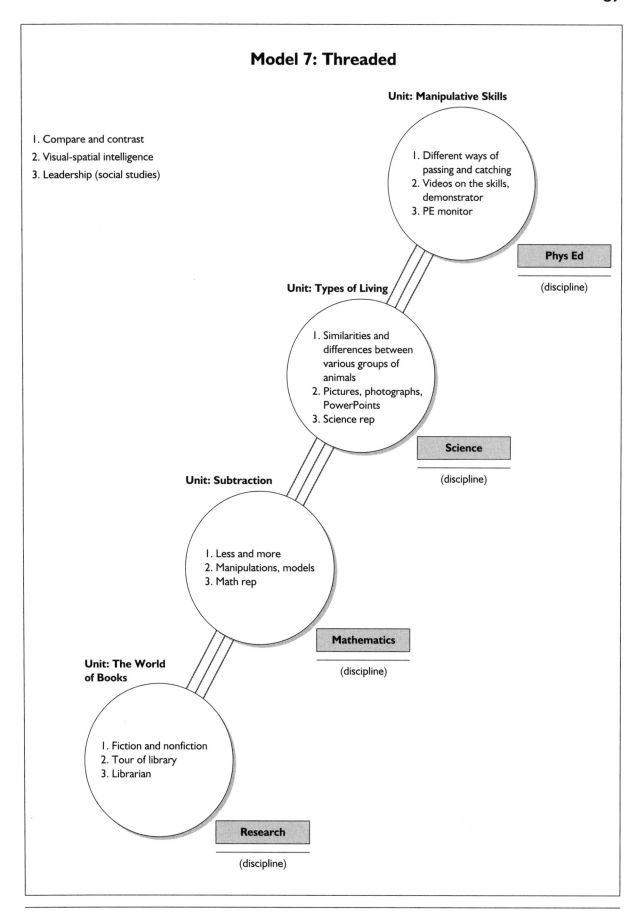

Model 7: Threaded

1. Compare and contrast
2. Visual-spatial intelligence
3. Leadership (social studies)

Unit: Manipulative Skills

1. Different ways of passing and catching
2. Videos on the skills, demonstrator
3. PE monitor

Phys Ed

(discipline)

Unit: Types of Living

1. Similarities and differences between various groups of animals
2. Pictures, photographs, PowerPoints
3. Science rep

Science

(discipline)

Unit: Subtraction

1. Less and more
2. Manipulations, models
3. Math rep

Mathematics

(discipline)

Unit: The World of Books

1. Fiction and nonfiction
2. Tour of library
3. Librarian

Research

(discipline)

Figure 7.8 Elementary School Example

Model 7: Threaded

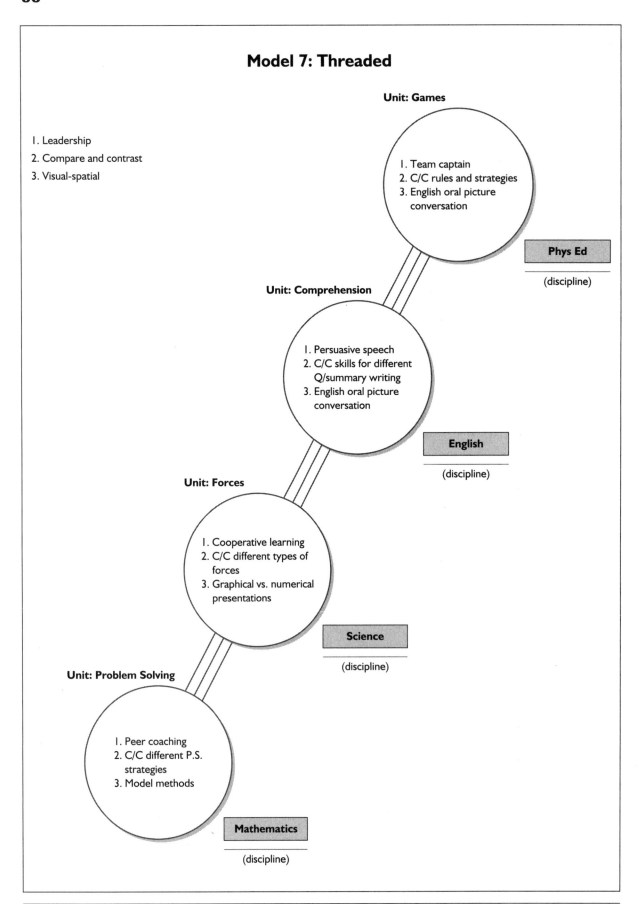

Figure 7.9 Middle School Example

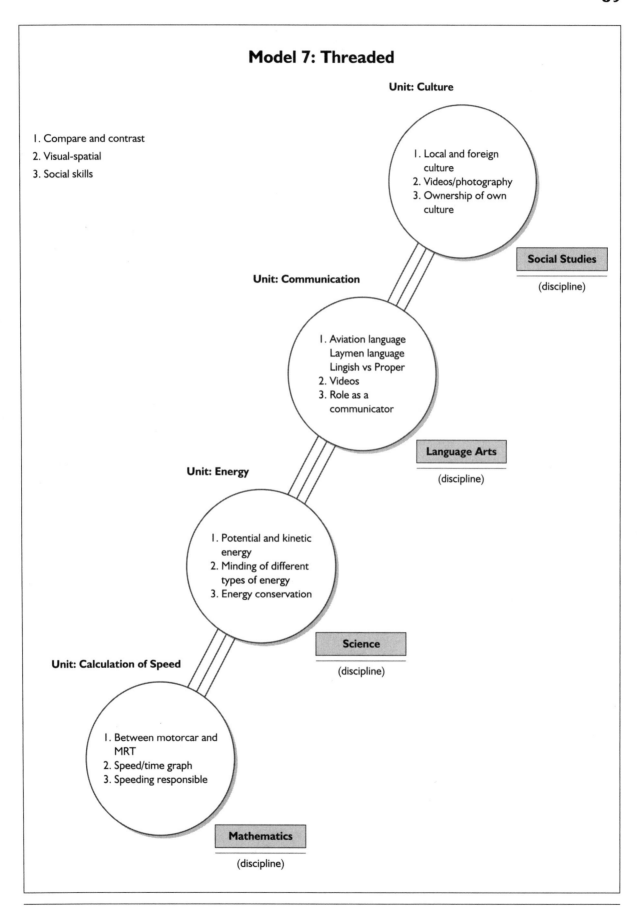

Figure 7.10   High School Example

HOW TO INTEGRATE THE CURRICULA WORKING WITH MODEL 7: THREADED

Essential Reasoning:

> *"We can dialogue from our respective classes and find shared concepts, skills, and attitudes that easily thread through various disciplines, giving students a shot of the skills, concepts, and attitudes in every class."*

Working as a cross-disciplinary team in the elementary, school, or high school, teachers meet to generate lists of the life skills students are expected to develop and use across many content areas. These are lists of the most common skills encountered in various disciplines. In the meeting, teachers focus on the many kinds of skills needed throughout life: thinking (predicting), social (reaching agreements), technology (spreadsheets), organizational (outlining), and habits of mind (perseverance) and strategies (problem solving, making decisions).

Once the life skills have been delineated, teachers select one skill to focus on for an agreed-upon period of time (week, month, term). They then build the skills into their lessons and look for teachable moments to thread the skills into the different subject areas.

Teachers meet periodically to discuss the impact of the threading in different classes.

Also, teachers can try threading several threads at once. For example: thinking—comparing and contrasting, communicating—debating, and writing—persuasiveness seem to go together.

Notes & Reflections
Model 7: Threaded

Essential Reasoning:

"We can dialogue from our respective classes and find shared concepts, skills, and attitudes that easily thread through various disciplines, giving students a shot of the skills, concepts, and attitudes in every class."

While this model of integrating the curricula by threading skills, concepts, and attitudes through various subject areas does require consensus from the team members, it is an integration model. The integration is natural, taking advantage of the teachable moments that occur in every lesson or unit.

At the same time, the curriculum integration is enduring because it is addressed in every discipline. It follows the old adage, "A little dab will do ya." In essence, a little taste of it in math, then again in science, and yet again in language class provides a broad reach across, and frequency of use in, various subjects.

In addition, there is no watering down of content in the respective disciplines. It is an amiable teaching model with positive outcomes for students. In the end, the threaded model addresses the metacurriculum, the set of skills, concepts, and attitudes that permeate all disciplines and even life situations far beyond the classroom.

This model seems natural for the elementary or self-contained classroom, yet is can also be the perfect fare for beginning curricula integration in more departmentalized middle and high school settings. In fact, it is the one model that is totally compatible with high school curriculum planning because it is so unobtrusive to the entire process.

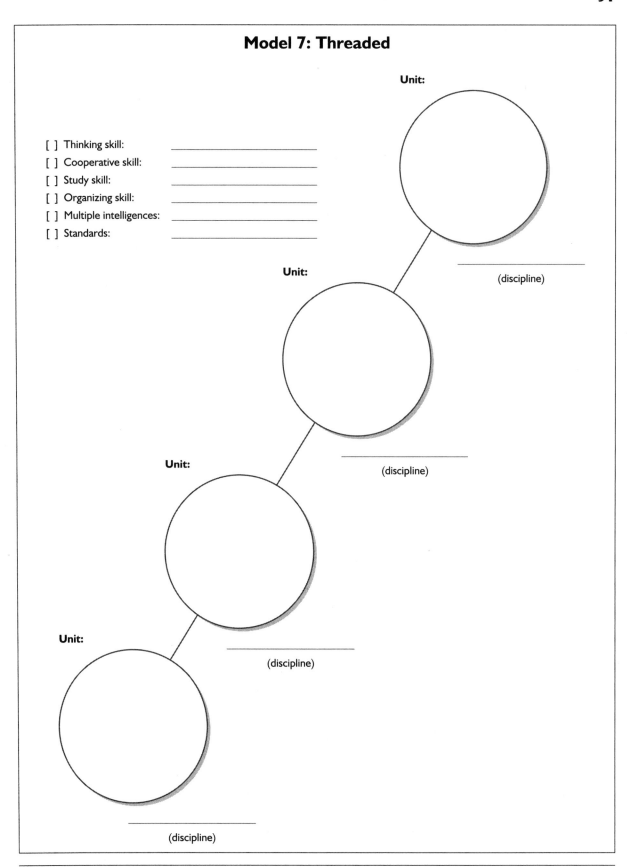

Figure 7.11 On Your Own

Model
8 Integrated

*Are we designing or
how might we design authentic
learning projects and performances
that integrate a number of disciplines?*

Kaleidoscope—new patterns and designs that use the basic elements of each discipline

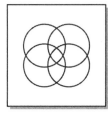

The integrated curricular model represents a cross-disciplinary approach similar to the shared model.

Example

In mathematics, science, social studies, fine arts, language arts, and practical arts, teachers look for patterns and approach content through these patterns in all the discipline areas.

"I call a complete and generous education that which fits [an individual] to perform justly, skillfully, and magnanimously all the offices, both private and public, of peace and war."
—John Milton

WHAT IS THE INTEGRATED MODEL?

The integrated curricular model represents a cross-disciplinary approach similar to the shared model. Although the traditional integrated model blends the four core disciplines by setting curricular priorities in each and finding the overlapping skills, concepts, and attitudes that occur in all four, it can be used with any number of disciplines. The model might include the arts as well as technology and other practical arts.

Yet in any version of the integrated model, just as in the simpler shared model, the integration is a result of sifting ideas out of subject matter content, not laying an idea over the subjects as in the webbed model. The integration sprouts from within the various disciplines, and matches are made among them as commonalities emerge. This is an inductive approach to curriculum integration, rather than a deductive approach as in the webbed model. It truly emerges from conversations and articulation across the disciplines. In fact, this model is the ultimate integration model because the patterns and themes truly do emerge from the various subject matter units. In essence, teachers continue to teach their content, but their focus takes on a bigger meaning that stretches to other content.

WHAT DOES IT LOOK LIKE?

In the middle or high school, the integrated curriculum is conceived as an interdisciplinary team struggles with an overloaded curriculum. Together, the team members decide to selectively abandon pieces from the traditional curriculum. Armed with content standards for the disciplines, the four (or more) team members begin to explore overlapping priorities and concepts that undergird their disciplines. One such overlap that they might discover early on is the concept of argument and evidence. It works well in mathematics, science, language arts, and social studies. It is a first step. It has that overarching quality of themes that makes it easy to use with myriad content.

In the elementary classroom, an integrated model that illustrates the critical elements of this approach is the literacy movement in which reading, writing, listening, and speaking skills spring from a literature-based program that taps all the energies of the learner and the disciplines. Literacy is learning that embraces an integrated curriculum as opposed to the more traditional, fragmented model in which each subject is addressed separately. Integrated models such as literacy are designed with the learner as the focus, while fragmented models are designed with content as the focus.

WHAT DOES IT SOUND LIKE?

What are the intersections of the various disciplines? What are the concepts, skills, and attitudes that bubble up from different subject matter content? Richards (1980) says, "Unless we educate for wholeness in person and wholeness of our Earth planet, we are not really intelligent. In our school subjects, we have an opportunity to study humankind as a family, and the Earth as the body of that family. We have the possibility of developing a curriculum which is like a map of its dreams and its history, a map of interconnections. Interdisciplinary methods try to avoid squeezing the life out of one part and blowing it up in another" (p. 11).

WHAT ARE THE ADVANTAGES?

A distinct advantage of the integrated model is the ease with which learners are introduced to the interconnectedness and interrelationships among various disciplines. The integrated model builds understanding across departments and fosters appreciation of staff knowledge and expertise. When successfully implemented, it approaches the ideal learning environment for an integrated day, externally, and for an integrated learner focus, internally. The integrated model also carries with it an inherent motivational factor as students and ideas gain momentum from class to class. The authentic projects and performances that result from this kind of deep integration are perfect platforms for integrating mathematics, science, social studies, and language arts with the visual, performing, and practical arts.

WHAT ARE THE DISADVANTAGES?

This is a sophisticated model that is difficult to implement fully. It requires highly skilled staff, confident in their knowledge of the content standards, skills, and attitudes that pervade their respective disciplines. In addition, the integrated model works best when interdepartmental teams have scheduled blocks of planning and teaching time in common, which often means major restructuring of schedules. To integrate curricula with explicit attention to the genuine conceptual priorities of each discipline requires the commitment of a myriad of resources.

WHEN IS THIS INTEGRATED MODEL USEFUL?

This model is most appropriately used with a cross-departmental team of volunteers who are willing to commit time and energy to the integration process. It is helpful to start with a small pilot project such as a three- to four-week unit. Summer curriculum writing time or designated release time during the semester is most likely necessary to fully explore this model.

After a pilot project is in place, further team commitment can be made. But a word of caution is needed here. It is not advisable for a school to adopt this model as a schoolwide reform without first giving it serious thought. Remember, committed volunteers across departments are the critical elements for this complex model. Eventually, as team members work together to learn about the other disciplines and other team members, the units can be planned for longer periods of time. This is a gradual process of building confidence and trust as team curriculum designers. However, after a team commits to the integrated model, the projects and performances that result often become unforgettable learning experiences for students.

Figures 8.1–8.4 are examples of completed integrated model integration exercises, and Figure 8.5 provides the opportunity for readers to record their own design for this model.

Model 8: Integrated
Readers' Theater

"The Heart of the Matter"

Narrator

Meanwhile, over the summer, meetings at the school are frequent and heated. Our teachers and the principal are exploring possibilities and looking for match-ups.

Sue Sum

I liked the webbed model we tried last year. But I sometimes felt like I was manipulating and contriving my content a bit. What if we tried a full-blown interdisciplinary team approach this year and looked for the natural overlaps?

Tom Time

I agree, Sue, but what if we only find a few guideline areas of overlap? How do we come to terms with that without artificially stretching our true priorities? Let's try the integrated approach in a pilot only. Maybe plan a three-week segment.

Bob Beaker

I think I know what you mean, Tom. We should first look at our individual content priorities and then sift out concepts, ideas, and attitudes that have overlapping elements. For example, my DNA unit. Aside from the technical information about genetic engineering, there are moral and ethical issues that overlap with social studies and language arts. There are also a number of mathematical concepts inherent to the DNA model.

Maria Novela

That's an exciting idea! I like coming from the heart of each discipline and then looking for the overlapping concepts. Let's go for it!

HOW TO INTEGRATE THE CURRICULA
WORKING WITH MODEL 8: INTEGRATED

Essential Reasoning:

"We use the integrated model as an inductive process for discerning the essential and enduring skills, concepts, and attitudes embedded within our disciplines. As we discuss our units of study, our minds close in on the overlapping ideas. The more we share, the more these commonalities simply bubble up from the content we are all addressing."

Similar to the shared model, in which two teachers look for overlapping ideas from their respective disciplines, the integrated model template (Figure 8.5) is

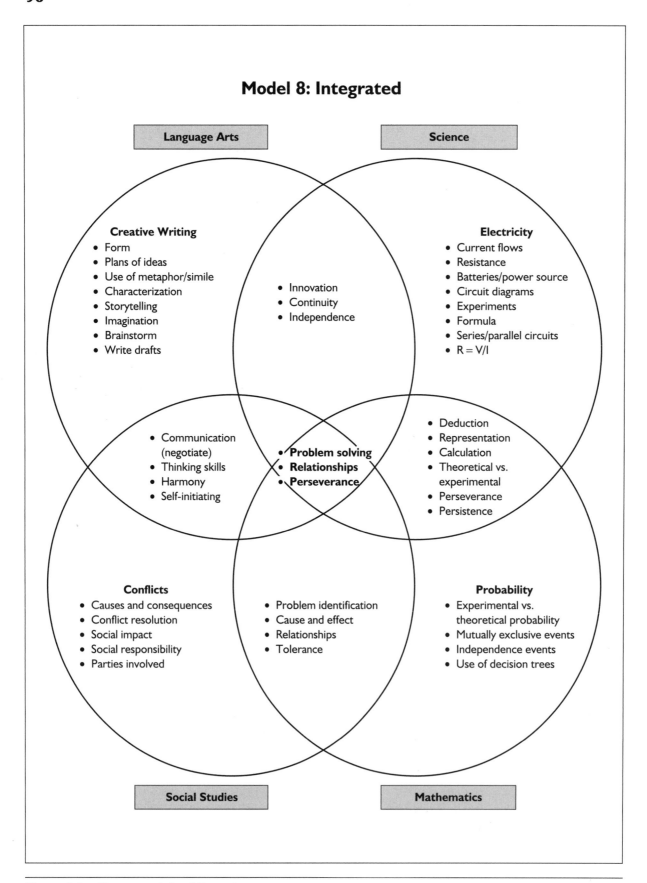

Model 8: Integrated

Language Arts

Science

Creative Writing
- Form
- Plans of ideas
- Use of metaphor/simile
- Characterization
- Storytelling
- Imagination
- Brainstorm
- Write drafts

- Innovation
- Continuity
- Independence

Electricity
- Current flows
- Resistance
- Batteries/power source
- Circuit diagrams
- Experiments
- Formula
- Series/parallel circuits
- $R = V/I$

- Communication (negotiate)
- Thinking skills
- Harmony
- Self-initiating

- **Problem solving**
- **Relationships**
- **Perseverance**

- Deduction
- Representation
- Calculation
- Theoretical vs. experimental
- Perseverance
- Persistence

Conflicts
- Causes and consequences
- Conflict resolution
- Social impact
- Social responsibility
- Parties involved

- Problem identification
- Cause and effect
- Relationships
- Tolerance

Probability
- Experimental vs. theoretical probability
- Mutually exclusive events
- Independence events
- Use of decision trees

Social Studies

Mathematics

Figure 8.1   Elementary School Example

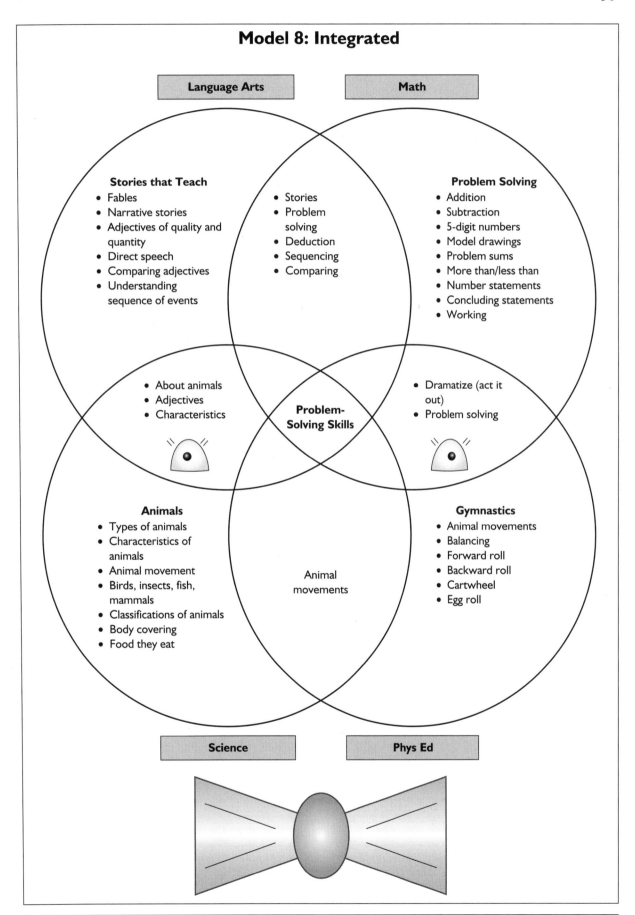

Figure 8.2 Elementary School Example

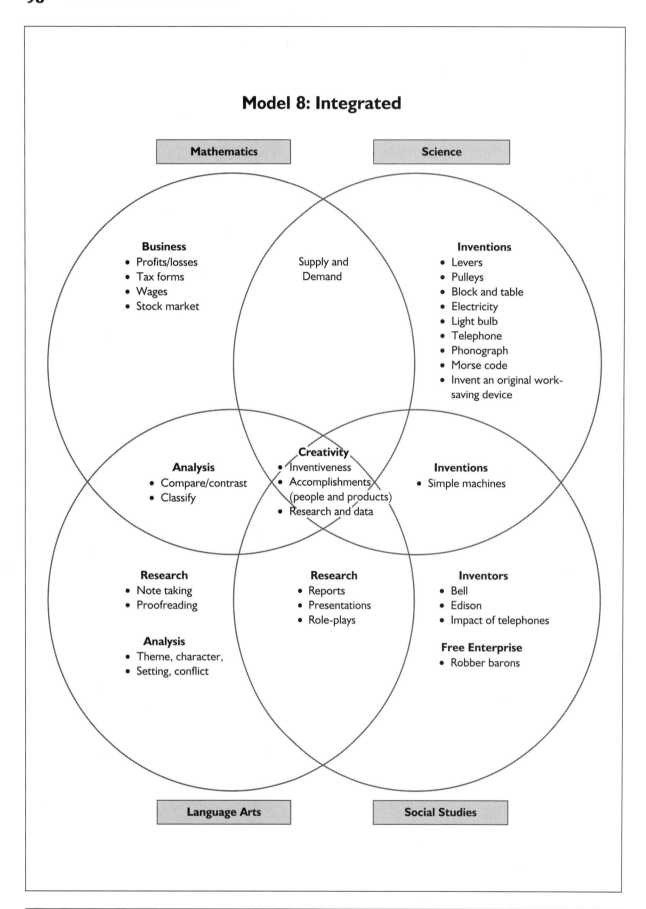

Figure 8.3   Middle School Example

Model 8: Integrated

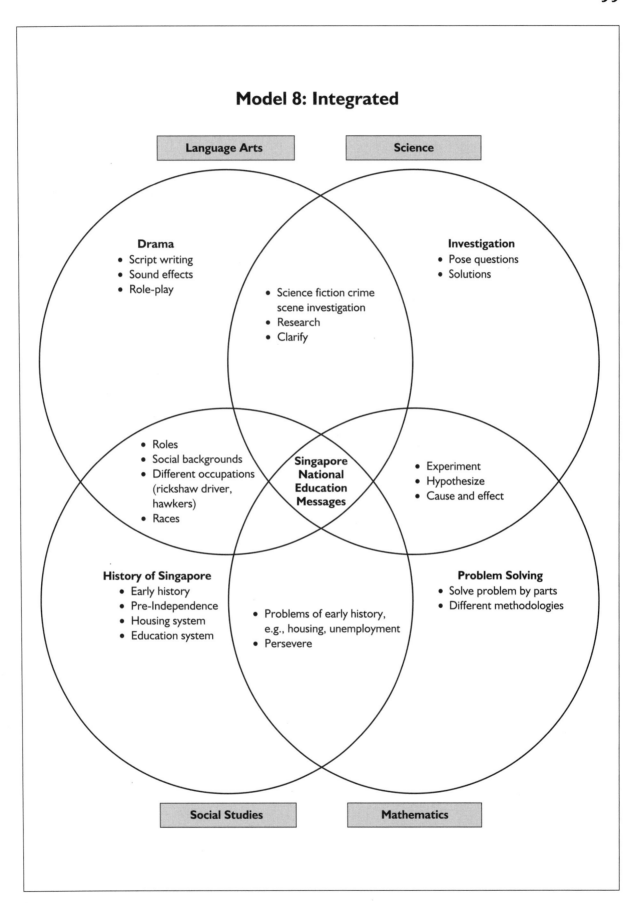

Language Arts

Science

Drama
- Script writing
- Sound effects
- Role-play

Investigation
- Pose questions
- Solutions

- Science fiction crime scene investigation
- Research
- Clarify

- Roles
- Social backgrounds
- Different occupations (rickshaw driver, hawkers)
- Races

Singapore National Education Messages

- Experiment
- Hypothesize
- Cause and effect

History of Singapore
- Early history
- Pre-Independence
- Housing system
- Education system

Problem Solving
- Solve problem by parts
- Different methodologies

- Problems of early history, e.g., housing, unemployment
- Persevere

Social Studies

Mathematics

Figure 8.4 High School Example

designed for a team of three or four teachers. As an interdisciplinary middle or high school or grade-level team, teachers take turns talking and writing about the units or topics in each of the disciplines.

Each teacher selects a unit of study for that term and shares in some detail what occurs during unit. While talking about the unit, he or she writes key words in the outer circle for that subject.

As the discussion progresses, the team members use an inductive approach and start to identify and label what bubbles up in the center. They look for overlaps and commonalities among the various subjects.

Once the team finds the life skills and big ideas that could serve as themes for all the subjects represented in the integrated unit, they proceed to develop essential questions from each discipline to drive the theme.

Notes & Reflections
Model 8: Integrated

Essential Reasoning:

"We use the integrated model as an inductive process for discerning the essential and enduring skills, concepts, and attitudes embedded within our disciplines. As we discuss our units of study, our minds close in on the overlapping ideas. The more we share, the more these commonalities simply bubble up from the content we are all addressing."

With content priorities in mind, team members look beyond the topics to the concepts, skills, and attitudes targeted in the separate disciplines. Armed with these basics, the team looks for overlapping ideas that emerged as common ground among the four disciplines.

The numerous similarities that naturally emerge from the content pieces may surprise the team members. It can be such an easy discussion to have because each teacher simply talked about his or her own content and the things addressed in the unit. No one needs to feel intimidated because no one is expected to know the others' content. It is a true learning experience as team members become privy to what other teachers are doing in their everyday lessons.

"We had no idea that there would be that many meaningful connections. We even commented that before the discussion that revolved around this model, we really did not know that much about what the other subject area teachers actually taught."

SOURCE: Adapted from a course taught by Kathleen Vehring, Carpentersville, IL.

Model 8: Integrated

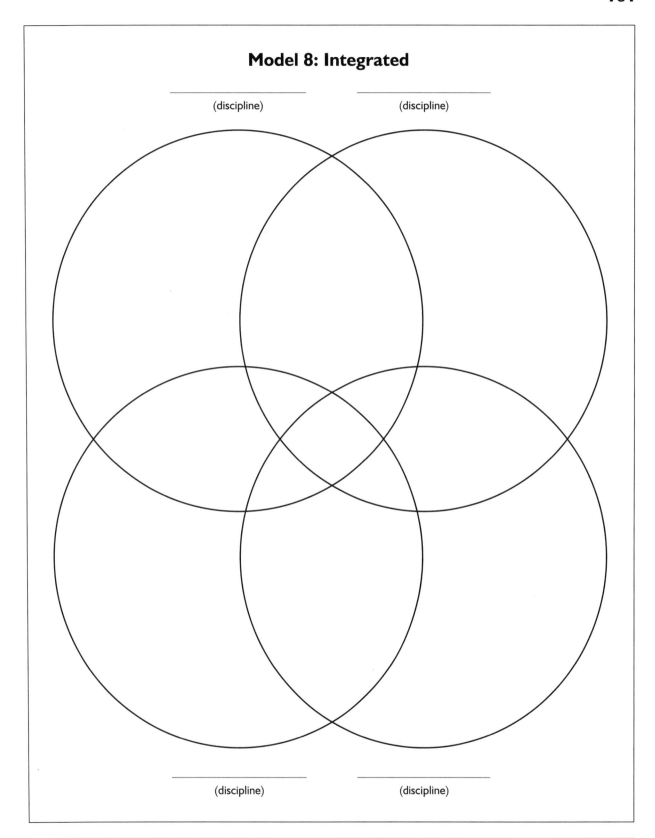

Figure 8.5 On Your Own

Immersed

*Are we or how are we using
learner-centered models in
which students have choices?*

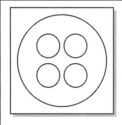

Microscope—intensely personal view that allows microscopic exploration as all content is filtered through lens of interest and expertise

The individual integrates all data, from every field and discipline, by funneling the ideas through his or her area of intense interest.

Example

A student or doctoral candidate has an area of expert interest and sees all learning through that lens.

"The one real object of education is to have a [person] in the condition of continually asking questions."

—Bishop Mondell Creighton

WHAT IS THE IMMERSED MODEL?

Aficionados, art students, prodigies, graduate students, doctoral candidates, and postdoctoral fellows are totally immersed in a field of study. The immersed model filters all curricular content learning through one microscopic lens. In this model of integrated curricula, the integration is internally and intrinsically accomplished by the learner with little or no extrinsic or outside intervention. It is real-world integration that naturally occurs as the learner reaches into the topic of interest and starts to find all kinds of marvelous connections.

WHAT DOES IT LOOK LIKE?

At the university level, a doctoral candidate is immersed in, for example, bio-chemistry. Her area of specialization is chemical bonding of substances. Even though her field is chemistry, she devours the software programs in computer science classes so she can analyze her data in simulated lab experiments, saving days of tedious lab work. She accepts an offer to learn patent law in order to protect her ideas for her company and to protect her company from liability cases. All learning paths are sparked by her passion for her field.

Likewise, a first grader writes incessantly about butterflies, bugs, spiders, insects, and creepy crawlies of all sorts. Her artwork is modeled on the symmetrical design of ladybugs and the patterns of butterflies. She counts, mounts, frames, and sings about them. Her interest in insect biology is already consuming her. The books she chooses reflect her internal integration of her interest in learning this subject.

WHAT DOES IT SOUND LIKE?

An immersed learner might say something like this: "I'm totally immersed in my work. It is a labor of love, and my laboratory is my life. It seems that everything I choose to pursue with any fervor is directly related to my intellectual interest." Just as the writer records notes and the artist makes sketches, the immersed learner is constantly making connections to his or her subject. With this self-directed, self-initiating learner, the teacher's mission often becomes one of getting out of the learner's way or finding ways to ignite the learning interest with myriad paths of discovery.

WHAT ARE THE ADVANTAGES?

The ultimate advantage is that integration must take place within the learner, which is exactly what is illustrated in this model. The learner is self-driven by an insatiable hunger to understand. "The more we know, the more we know we don't know" becomes an unhidden truth. As the student digs deeper into a field of interest, the related areas and new pathways seem unending. And the immersed learner exhibits phenomenal discipline as he or she develops this intense focus. Of course, another plus is that the connection making of this learner is often made explicit to other learners as the expert makes advances in the field.

WHAT ARE THE DISADVANTAGES?

The filtering of all ideas through a single microscopic lens may occur too prematurely or with too narrow a focus. Richness of experience and broad bases from which to review a specialization bring depth and dimension to the learner's perspective. A liberal background that cuts across the major disciplines provides the most fertile ground for enriching the learner's experience—the more varied, in fact, the better, at least early in the educational process. There is plenty of time to specialize later.

WHEN IS THIS IMMERSED MODEL USEFUL?

As teachers strive to differentiate curricula, they use the immersed model as part of various units of study. They direct students to choose an area of interest within a given framework and to pursue that area as a special project within the unit. When students select an area, they often become more invested in it and begin to integrate disciplines as they work on the project.

In other situations, such as career academies, high school students are already being asked to find their areas of strengths and choose a preliminary path of study that is connected to the careers in those stronger academic areas. Some select the art academy, while others prefer the health and science academy or the business academy. These learners practice the immersed model as they learn things through the lens of their career interest.

Immersion often begins as a hobby or a labor of love that directs the student's learning because of an intense interest in the area. Eventually, the student filters all learning through the lens of this interest, making natural connections across many disciplines.

Figures 9.1–9.3 are examples of completed immersion model integration exercises, and Figure 9.4 provides an opportunity for readers to record their own design for this model.

Model 9: Immersed
Readers' Theater

"The Ultimate Integrator"

Narrator

A graduate of the integrated curriculum school, and the university, tells his colleague . . .

Graduate

I'd been with the firm for five years as a chemical researcher and liked to just stick to the laboratory. But then I had to learn the CAD/CAM programs to use the technical equipment. The time I saved by using the computer simulations was unbelievable. Then I started spending a lot more time on the patenting process and started looking at patent law. Now the company wants me to go to law school.

Not only that, in order to deal with our Japanese manufacturers, I've started studying Japanese! I need some understanding of the language and culture. The learning never stops. Who knows what I'll get into next!

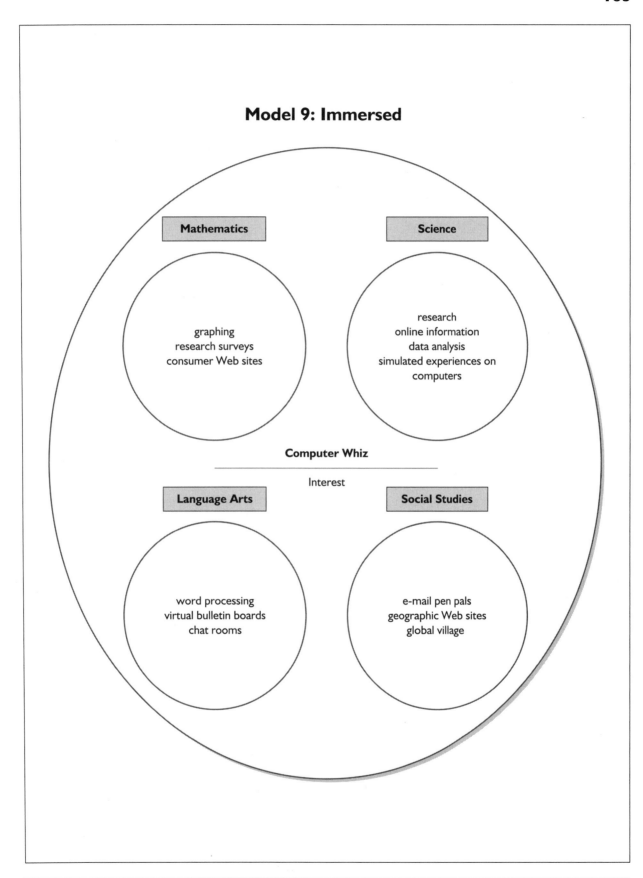

Figure 9.1   Elementary School Example

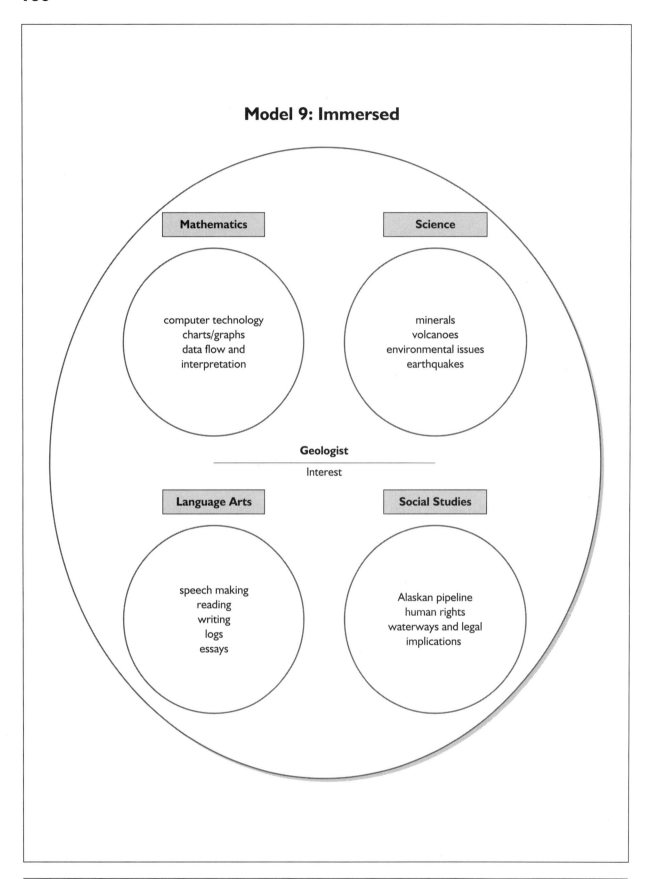

Figure 9.2 Middle School Example

Model 9: Immersed

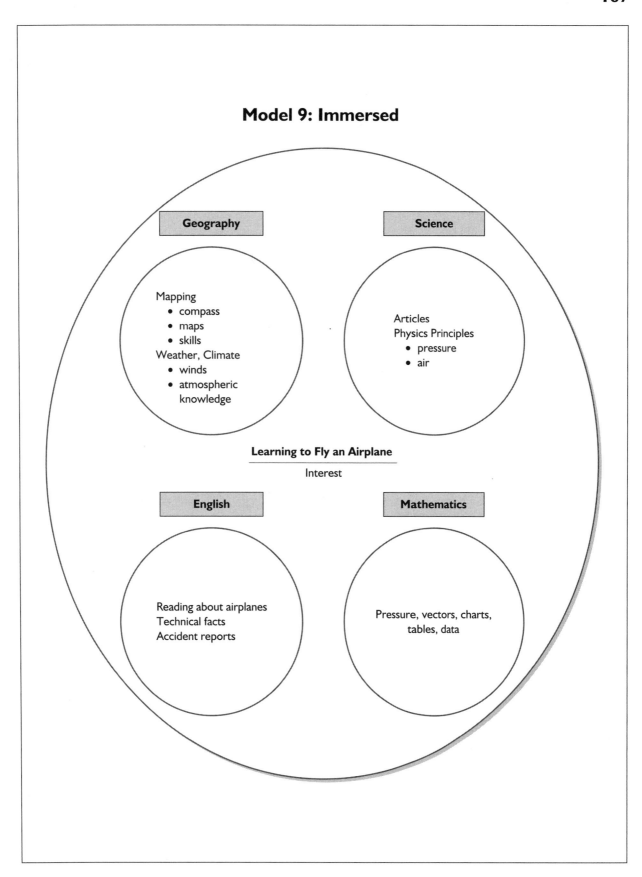

Figure 9.3   High School Example

HOW TO INTEGRATE THE CURRICULA WORKING WITH MODEL 9: IMMERSED

Essential Reasoning:

> *"I integrate many different skills, concepts, and attitudes from various subject matter content as I pursue my interest in _____."*

The natural integration of the various subjects for one student is represented in this template design (Figure 9.4). As the student pursues his or her personal area of intense interest, integration is naturally occurring. Use this template to plot the various disciplines involved as the student's investigation and curiosity drives the learning.

To utilize this immersed model, select one student or try it out on your own hobby, favorite pastime, or area of interest.

Through dialogue and discussion with a partner, take turns plotting the learning exposure to the various subjects through the selected lens of interest.

Use the samples as guides, but let the ideas flow to see how much integration actually occurs through the natural inquiry that is part of intrinsically motivated endeavors. This model's template offers a visual record of the integration that occurs.

Notes & Reflections
Model 9: Immersed

Essential Reasoning:

> *"I integrate many different skills, concepts, and attitudes from various subject matter content as I pursue my interest in _____."*

In the immersed model, students tend to funnel much authentic learning through their area of interest. Simply by following their consuming interest in a chosen area, they find that they are required to use many of the things they have learned throughout the disciplines. In fact, it is also the reason they learn many new things that they need in order to continue their journey. In essence, their overwhelming interest becomes the driving force for tackling new skills, concepts, and attitudes.

Students may find that they use a refined selection process that automatically screens input and seeks out the areas that have explicit and/or implicit connections to the things that they are most interested in.

The more expert they become, the more fine-tuned the selection process is. Their interest, their passion propels their learning in directions that they often do not anticipate. Yet with each new step they take, they learn and absorb whatever they need in order to foster their intense personal interest.

Model 9: Immersed

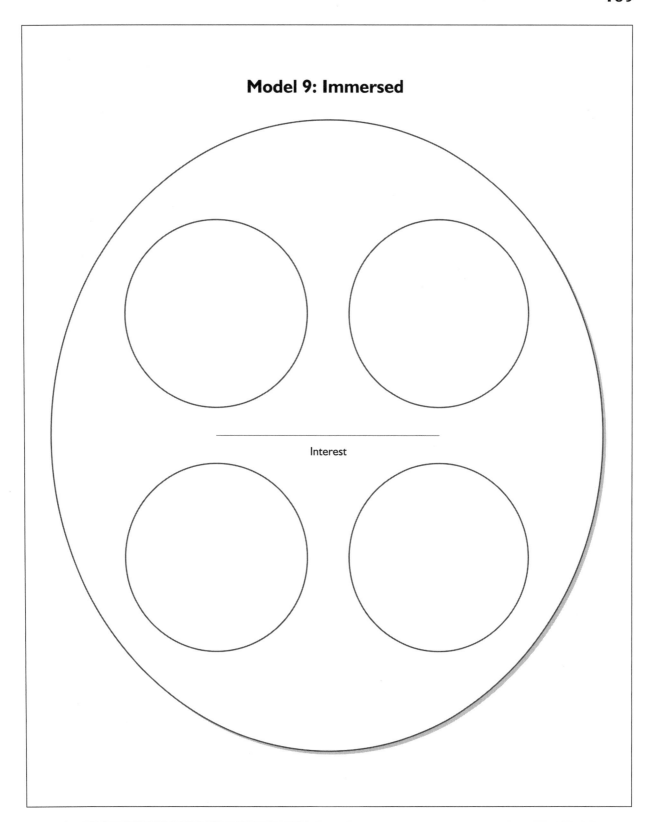

Interest

Figure 9.4 On Your Own

Model
10 Networked

*Are we or how are we
modeling real-world learning
that utilizes networks of experts?*

Prism—a view that creates
multiple dimensions and
directions of focus

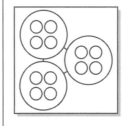

Example

An architect, while adapting the CAD/CAM
technology for design, networks with techno-
logical programmers and expands his or her
knowledge base, just as he or she had traditionally done with interior designers.

The networked model
of integrated learning
is an ongoing external
source of input,
forever providing new,
extended, and
extrapolated or
refined ideas.

"The education of a man is never completed until he dies."

—Robert E. Lee

WHAT IS THE NETWORKED MODEL?

The networked model of integrated learning involves ongoing external input
from other experts within and outside of the field of study and interest.
Learners' professional networks usually grow in obvious, and sometimes not so
obvious, directions. In the search for knowledge, learners come to depend on
their networks as a primary source of information that they must filter through
their own lens of expertise and interest.

In the networked model of integration, unlike in the earlier models, learners direct the integration process through self-selection of the needed networks.
Only the learners themselves, knowing the intricacies and dimensions of their
field, can target the necessary resources. This model, like the others, develops
and grows over time as needs propel learners in new directions.

WHAT DOES IT LOOK LIKE?

This model of networked integration is seen to a limited extent in the elementary school. Imagine a fifth grader who has maintained a keen interest in Native Americans since his toddler days of playing "Cowboys and Indians." His passion for Native American lore leads him to historical readings—both fiction and nonfiction. His family, well aware of his intrigue with Native Americans, hears about an archeological dig that recruits youngsters to participate in the dig as part of a summer program offered by a local college. As a result of the boy attending this summer camp, he meets people in a number of fields: an anthropologist, a geologist, an archeologist, an illustrator, and a student of the fine arts who was hired to represent the dig in drawings. This learner's networks are already taking shape. His natural interest has led him to others in the field who offer various levels of knowledge and insight that extend his learning.

WHAT DOES IT SOUND LIKE?

The networked model sounds like a three- or four-way conference call that provides various avenues of exploration and explanation. Although these diverse ideas may not come all at once, the networked learner is open to multiple modes of input as divergent components are sifted and sorted to suit the need. This model sounds like the network news—pulling in pictures and stories from around the globe. The network is much like a satellite beaming signals here and there and receiving signals from everywhere.

WHAT ARE THE ADVANTAGES?

The advantages of the networked model are many. This integrated learning approach is extremely proactive in nature, with learners initiating searches and following the newly emerging paths. Learners are stimulated with relevant information, skills, or concepts that move their learning along. The advantages of this model, however, cannot be imposed on learners, but rather must emerge from within. But mentors can and do provide the necessary support to encourage this sophisticated stage of learning.

WHAT ARE THE DISADVANTAGES?

The disadvantages of the networked model are familiar to those who have developed many diverse interests in their labors of love. It is easy to get side-tracked into one of the tangential ideas. It is also possible to get in over one's head. A particular path may seem inviting and useful, but may suddenly become overwhelming; the benefits no longer outweigh the price one has to pay. Another drawback is that the networked model, if taken to extremes, can spread interests too thin and dilute a concentrated effort.

WHEN IS THIS NETWORKED MODEL USEFUL?

This model, like the immersed model, often moves the onus of integration to learners rather than to outside instructional designers. However, it is an appropriate model to present to motivated learners. Tutors or mentors often suggest networking to extend the learners' horizons or provide a needed perspective. Of course, many times this model simply expands naturally from learners' inherent interest and motivation.

As networks evolve, serendipitous connections appear along the way. Often, these accidental findings propel learners into new depths in the field or lead to the creation of a more specialized field. One such example is the field of genetics, which has developed an area known as genetic engineering. This unfolding of a field is really the result of immersed expert learners networking with other immersed expert learners.

A more explicit example of the networked model is also used in larger high schools. As schools move to the small schools concept and create career academies, students are often expected to network with businesses in their chosen fields. This networking often leads to apprenticeships and/or internships within the career areas of interest. Of course, networking across various disciplines occurs as a natural part of this process.

Figures 10.1–10.3 are examples of completed networked model integration exercises, and Figure 10.4 provides the opportunity for readers to record their own design for this model.

Model 10: Networked
Readers' Theater

"Out There!"

Narrator

Years later . . . a graduate of the integrated school is on a conference call with two network experts, a cognitive psychologist and a computer programmer.

Lucy Librarian

I think of myself as a librarian. That was my training—library sciences. But as a doctoral candidate in the area of artificial intelligence, I need to network with others in highly technical fields. I am searching for a program to help simulate a cognitive search for information.

Sy Kee

What we know about how the brain works can be represented in the diagrams I sent you. Also, by scripting the talk-aloud monitoring of subjects, I think you'll be able to see patterns of connection making. If we put our heads together, this will start to make sense.

Connie Computo

It's hard to duplicate the insightful connections made by the human brain, but the randomness in the procedures can be programmed in. I will need explicit details from you, Lucy, about how we make those connections in the human brain.

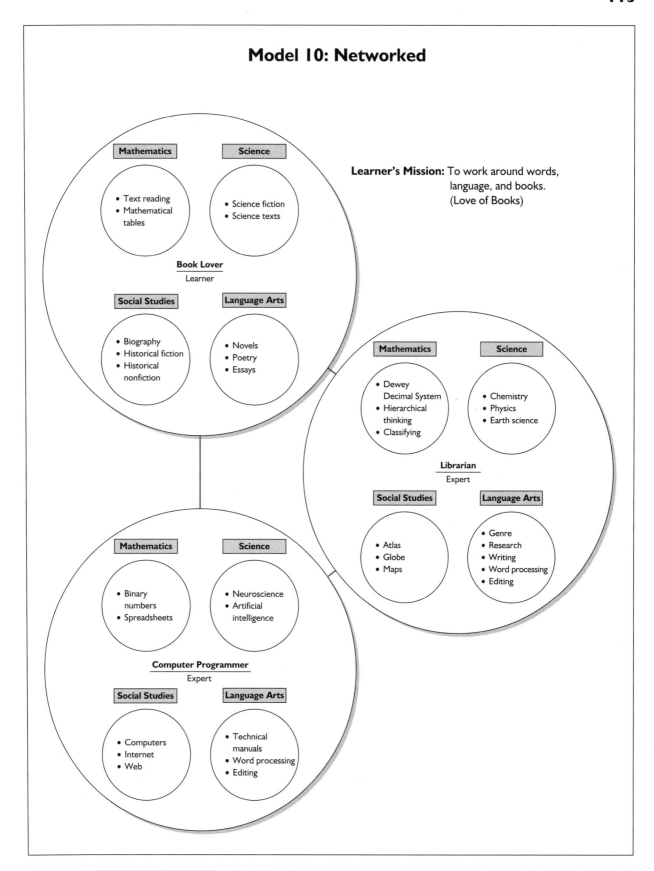

Figure 10.1   Elementary School Example

Model 10: Networked

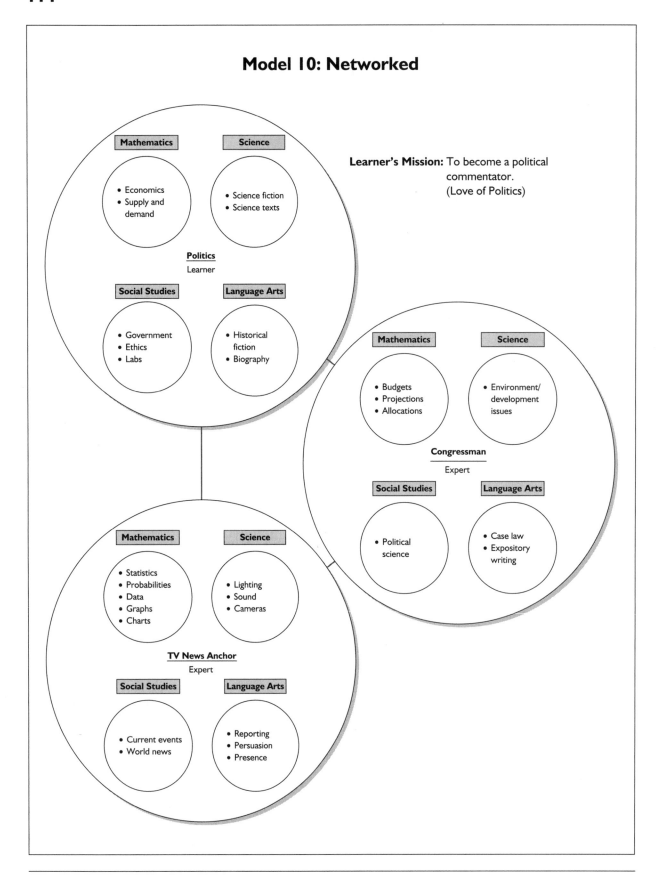

Learner's Mission: To become a political commentator. (Love of Politics)

Figure 10.2 Middle School Example

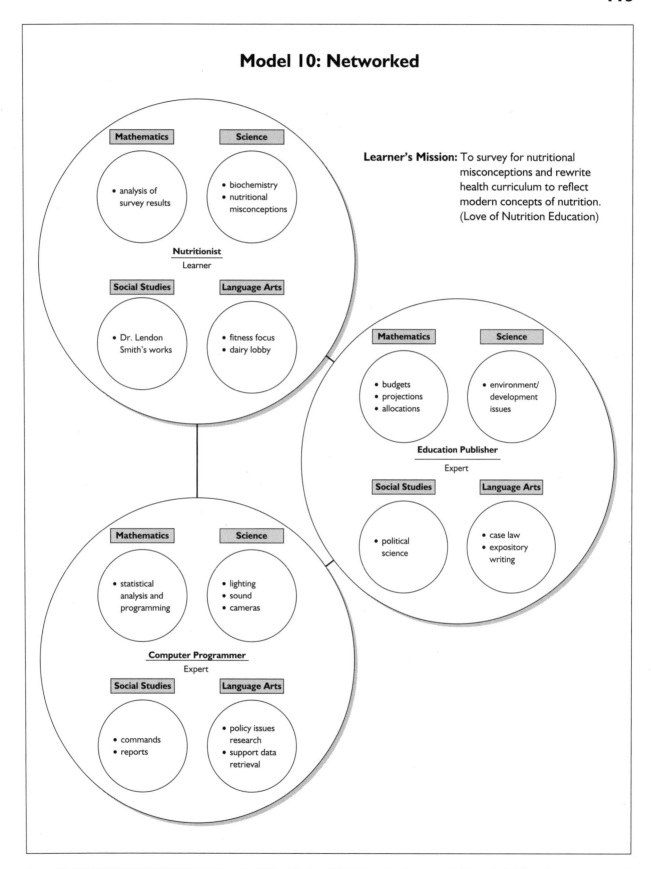

Figure 10.3   High School Example

HOW TO INTEGRATE THE CURRICULA WORKING WITH MODEL 10: NETWORKED

Essential Reasoning:

> *"I network with others, various experts in their field of study, as I explore all aspects of my area of interest."*

To work with the networked model, the teacher thinks of a passion, a labor of love, an area of intense interest that one student exhibits. The teacher might work with his or her own focus as a way to start using the template for this model (Figure 10.4).

Then, the teacher plots the path of networking opportunities for that student as he or she pursues this area of interest. As the student searches for information about the interest, myriad opportunities arise for the student to network with others, whether they be experts in the field or other colleagues pursuing the same interest. The student may also find print or electronic resources that lead to blogs or other connections.

To use the template (Figure 10.4), record the connected learning experiences that result, or might result, from the original seed of interest. Note how an interdisciplinary approach is inherent in this kind of natural pursuit of learning. This is the ultimate integration that takes place in the mind of the learner.

Notes & Reflections
Model 10: Networked

Essential Reasoning:

> *"I network with others, various experts in their field of study, as I explore all aspects of my area of interest."*

When learners have a special interest area that has become a passion, they naturally seek others who know more about this area than they do. Learners find themselves searching out experts, both inside and outside the field, to extend and enrich the field.

Learners look for expertise from those immersed in the same field of study as they are. They may want a mentor to push their thinking and awareness of all angles. They seek those who have insights and inclinations that they might otherwise miss.

Interestingly, learners may also find themselves networking with people in other fields as their journey leads them in many directions and toward unintended outcomes. These people are experts in their fields and are welcome colleagues engaged along the way. The richness of these encounters cannot be overstated. Their impact on the entire pursuit is invaluable.

In brief, this networked model is perhaps the most inherently authentic model of curriculum integration because it involves the practical pursuit of learning about a deeply consuming area of personal interest.

Model 10: Networked

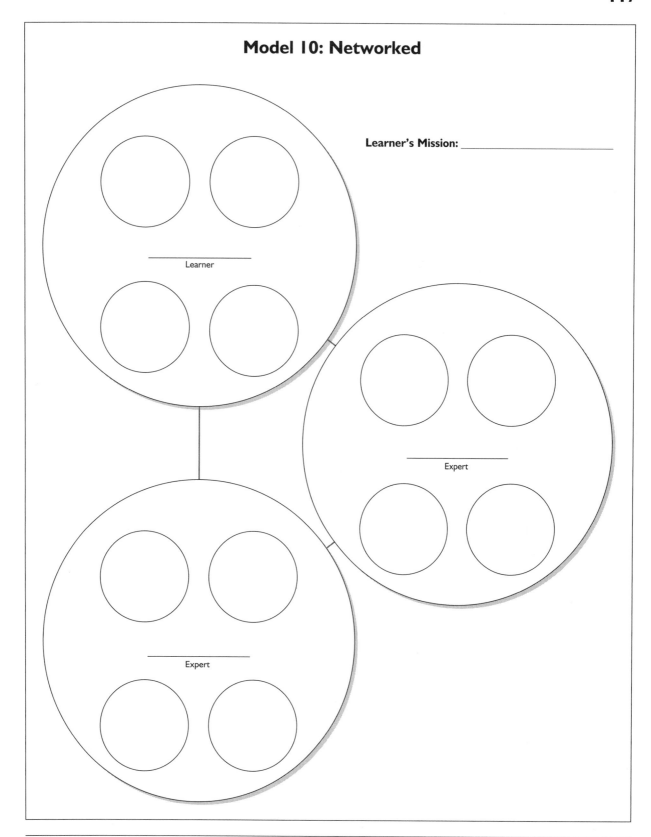

Figure 10.4 On Your Own

Appendix

Assessing Curriculum Integration

Units of Study

APPRAISING CURRICULUM INTEGRATION

The question about how to assess integrated curriculum is often on teachers' minds as they move toward more integrated curriculum models. While this is a fair question and appears to be quite straightforward, it is actually fairly ambiguous. Is the question about assessing the quality of the curriculum integration unit itself, or is it about how to assess students who are involved in the curriculum integration unit?

The answer is that it is about both. Teachers want some yardstick with which to measure the unit of study that has been developed around the idea of a more coherent, more connected way of addressing the curriculum. Yet they also want and need ways to assess the learning that occurs when students are immersed in integrated curriculum projects and performances.

In the subsequent discussion, two sets of rubrics are presented. First comes a scoring rubric that helps teachers look at the integrity of the curriculum integration unit. This is followed by two examples to illustrate how teams might analyze a unit for curriculum integrity and instructional quality. The second set of rubrics includes viable tools for evaluating student work; they provide various criteria that can serve as assessment areas for student learning. One rubric provides a general assessment of student learning for the entire unit of study, and two others provide discipline-specific rubrics as models for individual teacher assessment of student work in their subject.

In the end, both kinds of rubrics provide distinct pivot points for discussions. These conversations often lead to deeper understanding of how to develop quality curriculum integration and foster an examination of how to assess and appraise student work within a unit. After all, grades and rankings are a necessary evil of the school curriculum.

APPRAISING THE INTEGRITY OF THE BREADTH AND DEPTH OF THE CURRICULUM INTEGRATION UNIT

To fully examine the quality of a curriculum integration unit, five characteristics are used: relevance, richness, relatedness, rigor, and recursion. Let's unpack the meaning of these critical elements as they apply to the curriculum integration process and as products of a more integrated approach to curriculum. Then we'll proceed to the sample rubric and the two examples to see how these elements are applied to curriculum integration units.

Relevance

Students expect learning to be meaningful and often search for the reason that they are learning something and how they will use it. Integrated units are developed for that very reason: to make the learning purposeful. The intent is to make learning opportunities more personally relevant by incorporating life experiences and real-world applications.

Richness

Richness involves multilayering. It is about units of study that address the eight multiple intelligences delineated by Gardner (1983, 1999): visual-spatial, verbal-linguistic, intrapersonal-self, interpersonal-social, musical-rhythmic, mathematical-logical, naturalist-physical world, and bodily-kinesthetic. Richness is about ambiguity and wholeness; it is about depth and texture. Richness enhances the unit with its robustness.

Relatedness

Relatedness refers to natural hookups and connections across the various disciplines. It is about how broadly the unit reaches into the various disciplines in genuine and interwoven ways. Relatedness is really about how cohesive the unit is, how tightly it is designed, and how many genuine overlaps are evidenced across multiple content areas.

Rigor

Rigor is about complexity and the intricacies of higher-order thinking that are inherent in the unit of study. Rigor does not mean that the work is hard, but rather that it is of high quality and complexity, that it requires the thoughtfulness and mindfulness of problem solving and decision making. Rigor dictates expert performances and results in multilayered products.

Recursion

Recursion is about how often the themes and big ideas recur in the unit as well as in other school and life circumstances. Themes of the highest integrity are those that recur often and in various ways in subject matter content and real-life situations. Recursion is evidence that the themes are worthy, worldly, and widely influential.

Sample Rubric

A scoring rubric has three elements that matter: standard, criteria, and indicators of quality. The standard for a curriculum integration unit of study is the exemplar of curriculum design that utilizes big-idea themes or life skills in student-centered learning experiences. The criteria delineate specific critical components that are targeted in the learning experience. The indicators of quality represent the range of quality, from low to high, that is judged in the assessment of the unit.

The rubric developed to appraise the integrity of quality of a curriculum integration unit applies the five elements described earlier in this discussion:

- relevance
- richness
- relatedness
- rigor
- recursion

These five elements are the target criteria that are juxtaposed with key quality indicators:

- *Not Yet!* Limited progress, needs help, does not meet standards
- *On Our Way!* Developing, emerging, on the brink, almost meets standards
- *This Is It!* In the zone, competent, good job, meets standards
- *Above and Beyond!* Exceptional, superior, proficient, exceeds standards

The resulting matrix allows for a rating of the entire curriculum integration unit. As a unit is designed and implemented, the key players consistently look at the five elements and try to score them appropriately.

Note in Figure A.1 that each criterion can be scored horizontally across the row, using the quality indicator headings as a guide. For example:

- Relevance is rated from "inert knowledge" to "forecasted utilization."
- Richness moves from "contrived to fit" to "breadth, depth, and integrity."
- Relatedness spans from "no obvious connections across disciplines" to "natural, genuine connections to life situations."
- Rigor ranges from "recall and regurgitation" to "applying intricate complexities."
- Recursion runs from "singular opportunity for concept/skill development" to "transfer with creative ambiguity."

Naturally, the more scores that fall on the right side of the matrix as each criterion is analyzed and examined, the higher the quality of the curriculum integration unit. Utilizing this kind of analysis affords the design team several opportunities to look closely at the unit's integrity. They can review the unit in the design stage, before it is unveiled, during implementation, and finally after it has been completed and student learning is addressed.

Criteria for Robust Integrated Units	Not Yet!	On Our Way!	This Is It!	Above and Beyond!
RELEVANCE • Meaningful • Purposeful • Life experiences • Real	Inert knowledge	Relates conceptually	Real-world applications	Forecasted utilization
RICHNESS • Multilayered • Ambiguous • Multiple intelligences • Depth of content	Contrived to fit	Authentic dimensions	Breadth and depth across intelligences	Breadth, depth, and integrity
RELATEDNESS • Genuine overlaps • Intentional • Natural hookups across disciplines	No obvious connections across disciplines	Superficial connections across disciplines	Natural, genuine connections across disciplines	Natural, genuine connections to life situations
RIGOR • Problem solving • Decision making • Higher-order thinking • Expert performance	Pour and store: recall and regurgitation	Challenge: follow rigorous procedures	Struggle: getting stuck and getting unstuck	Applying intricate complexities
RECURSION • Recurs • Applies • Threads through and carries over • Flops back and returns to	Singular opportunity for concept/skill development	Multiple opportunities for concept/skill development	Transfer of skills and concepts to novel situations through problem solving	Transfer with creative ambiguity

Figure A.1   Rubric for Integrated Curriculum Units of Study

SOURCE: Adapted from "Curriculum Possibilities in a 'Post-Future,'" by W. Doll, 1993, *Journal of Curriculum and Supervision, 8*(4), pp. 270–292.

Example Rubric #1: Social Studies/History Unit: How Does War Create Peace?

Figure A.2 presents a rubric for determining the quality of an integrated unit called How Does War Create Peace?

A quick glance horizontally across the rows of Figure A.2 reveals the kind of discussion that might occur. The questions, of course, can only be answered fully when an actual, fully developed curriculum unit is reviewed. Yet the process can be revealed here in brief. For example, when looking at the full criteria for the How Does War Create Peace? unit, note the possible explanations.

Relevance

If the unit is presented as "inert knowledge" rather than a "genuine comparison to a current conflict," it would be scored low. The true relevance of a unit can be judged by the authentic involvement of students and their personalization of the unit and its many elements.

Criteria for Robust Integrated Units	Not Yet!	On Our Way!	This Is It!	Above and Beyond!
RELEVANCE • Meaningful • Purposeful • Life experiences • Real	Inert knowledge **WWII as an event**	Relates conceptually **War as an historical area**	Real-world applications **Concept of conflict**	Forecasted utilization **Genuine comparison to current conflict**
RICHNESS • Multilayered • Ambiguous • Multiple intelligences • Depth of content	Contrived to fit **Pencil-and-paper tasks and tests**	Authentic dimensions **Simulate the war**	Breadth and depth across intelligences **Develop a museum**	Breadth, depth, and integrity **Develop dynamic, fluid, and interactive memorial**
RELATEDNESS • Genuine overlaps • Intentional • Natural hookups across disciplines	No obvious connections across disciplines **WWII as isolated event**	Superficial connections across disciplines **WWII as focus for related projects**	Natural, genuine connections across disciplines **War as concept in economics, literature, and science**	Natural, genuine connections to life situations **Real-world cohesive endeavors**
RIGOR • Problem solving • Decision making • Higher-order thinking • Expert performance	Pour and store: recall and regurgitation **WWII: show and tell**	Challenge: follow rigorous procedures **WWII: cause and effect**	Struggle: getting stuck and getting unstuck **WWII: problem solving what-if's**	Applying intricate complexities **Complex hypotheses**
RECURSION • Recurs • Applies • Threads through and carries over • Flops back and returns to	Singular opportunity for concept/skill development **Conflict in context of work**	Multiple opportunities for concept/skill development **Conflict across contexts**	Transfer of skills and concepts to novel situations through problem solving **Conflict experienced in the process**	Transfer with creative ambiguity **Ambiguous conflicts of interest**

Figure A.2   Rubric for "How Does War Create Peace?" Integrated Unit

Richness

If the unit strives to "develop a dynamic, fluid, and interactive memorial," it is more likely to score at the highest end of the rubric. This is determined by the amount and quality of multimodal opportunities for differentiated learning and by the genuine performances and products that result.

Relatedness

If the unit connects various disciplines in "real-world cohesive endeavors," it would score high in the area of relatedness. This concept of interrelatedness is signaled by the number of real overlaps across various disciplines as the projects evolve.

Rigor

If the unit settles for a "show and tell" approach as evidence of student participation and learning, rather than generating "complex hypotheses," the element of rigor would rank at the low end. Rigor is not about how hard the tasks are, but rather how complex and intricate the endeavors become.

Recursion

If theme of conflict moves toward genuine, real-world "ambiguous conflicts of interests," the unit would score quite high in terms of recursion. The recursiveness becomes obvious as the major themes seem to crop up, over and over again, with connections to life outside of the schoolhouse walls.

Example Rubric #2: Science/Math/Language Arts Unit: Bridging the Way

Figure A.3 presents a rubric for determining the quality of an integrated unit of study called Bridging the Way.

Again, a quick glance horizontally across the rows reveals the kind of discussion that might occur in terms of this unit's quality.

Relevance

If the unit demonstrates personal meaning, and the students show evidence of owning the theme by developing real products and performances based on "metaphorical" understanding of the bridges concept, it is deemed highly relevant.

Richness

If the entire unit demonstrates strong, reliable, and valid evidence of multimodal teaching and learning, with bridges of layered depth and complexity, that is characteristic of a richness in the approach.

Relatedness

If the unit connects to various disciplines with integrity (e.g., language arts: conjunctive, prepositional bridges; science: bones, ligaments, and muscles as bridges; social studies: economic, political bridges; business: organizational bridges), it is judged to have high quality in terms of relatedness.

Rigor

If the unit focuses solely on real bridges with drawings, model building, and presentations on the infrastructure of the country, it may result in a high level of interest from students, yet is seems somewhat limited in its integrative themes and would be rated low to medium in terms of rigor.

Recursion

If there is extensive evidence of the critical threads in all disciplines being involved and related to real-life situations in universal and generalizing ways, the unit scores high in recursion.

Criteria for Robust Integrated Units	Not Yet!	On Our Way!	This Is It!	Above and Beyond!
RELEVANCE (Real)	Inert knowledge **Bridges (types)**	Relates conceptually **Bridges in art/ architecture and design**	Real-world applications **Concept of bridges**	Forecasted utilization **Read a metaphorical bridge of all aspects of life**
RICHNESS (Multidimensional)	Contrived to fit **Pencil-and-paper tasks and tests about types of bridges**	Authentic dimensions **Design, sketch, paint, and draw bridges**	Breadth and depth across intelligences **A developed exhibition of models of bridges**	Breadth, depth, and integrity **Multimodal bridges, from verbal bridge to vertical bridge**
RELATEDNESS (Connected)	No obvious connections across disciplines **Bridges of the world**	Superficial connections across disciplines **Bridges as structures**	Natural, genuine connections across disciplines **Bridges as concept in economics, literature, science, development, etc.**	Natural, genuine connections to life situations **Bridges to and from all aspects of our lives (six degrees of separation)**
RIGOR (Higher-order thinking)	Pour and store: recall and regurgitation **Name, locate, and describe bridges**	Challenge: follow rigorous procedures **Bridges: making and breaking**	Struggle: getting stuck and getting unstuck **Bridges: problem solving what-if's**	Applying intricate complexities **Ambiguous bridges that make us think**
RECURSION (Transfer)	Singular opportunity for concept/skill development **Bridges as architecture**	Multiple opportunities for concept/skill development **Bridges across contexts (conjunctions, transitions)**	Transfer of skills and concepts to novel situations through problem solving **Personally relevant bridges**	Transfer with creative ambiguity **Bridging concepts that recur universally**

Figure A.3   Rubric for "Bridging the Way" Integrated Unit

ASSESSING THE EFFECTIVENESS OF THE UNIT IN TERMS OF STUDENT ACHIEVEMENT

Assessing the effectiveness of the curriculum integration unit in terms of student learning involves another set of criteria and quality indicators that comprise the elements of a scoring rubric. One rubric may serve as an assessment for the entire unit, yet it seems prudent that each discipline create its own scoring rubric. In this way, each teacher, representing a particular subject, is able to delineate specific areas of assessment appropriate to that discipline. Thus, students might receive a grade on the entire project and/or a separate grade for each discipline or subject area. In the following pages, there is an example of a general rubric that might be used for one class and one grade. There are also samples of two discipline-specific rubrics, one for history and one for language arts.

General Rubric

In this general rubric for a robust curriculum integration unit (see Figure A.4), there are four distinct criteria:

- content knowledge
- process skills
- enduring learnings
- serendipities

These criteria are juxtaposed with quality indicators that allow the teacher and student to judge the work from lower quality to higher quality. As described before, these four quality indicators comprise the following:

- *Not Yet!* Limited progress, needs help, does not meet standards
- *On Our Way!* Developing, emerging, on the brink, almost meets standards
- *This Is It!* In the zone, competent, good job, meets standards
- *Above and Beyond!* Exceptional, superior, proficient, exceeds standards

The resulting matrix allows for a rating of the entire curriculum integration unit. As a curriculum unit is designed and implemented, the key players consistently look at the four elements and try to score them appropriately. Content knowledge is rated from "little evidence" to "meaningful application." Process skills are scored from "disorganized work with little evidence of organization and little problem solving or decision making" to "outstanding organization, problem solving, and decision making with creative ideation." Enduring learnings are ranked from "unaware of concepts, big ideas, and themes" to "conceptual understandings are generalized and applied." Serendipities range from "not consciously aware of unexpected results" to "highly positive unintended outcomes applied and used."

The following two discipline-specific units are intended to be previewed in the same way as the general rubric (see Figures A.5 and A.6). Move horizontally across the rows of criteria, and judge the student learning accordingly.

History Rubric

Description of Criteria

- Historical content: facts, dates, events, and major themes
- Evidence of research: search with volume, variety, and validity
- Historical inferences: higher-order thinking (making inferences, drawing conclusion, finding relevant implications)
- Completion of project: quality project displayed and described with elaboration

Language Arts Rubric

Description of Criteria

- Content knowledge: sound grasp of the language arts content
- Persuasive essay: appropriate prototype executed
- Evidence of literacy references: seminal references cited properly
- Application of skills: utilization of language arts skills and mechanics

Criteria for Evidence of Student Learning	Not Yet!	On Our Way!	This Is It!	Above and Beyond!
Content Knowledge • Subject matter • Content • Target disciplines	Little evidence of content knowledge	Knowledge emerging	Competent and robust understanding	Meaningful applications of content knowledge
Process Skills • Organization • Research • Problem solving • Decision making • Creative ideation	Disorganized work with little evidence of organization and little problem solving or decision making	Some evidence of organization, yet little problem solving or decision making	Sound organization with problem solving and decision making	Outstanding organization, problem solving, and decision making, with creative ideation
Enduring Learning • Subject matter • Content • Target disciplines	Unaware of concepts, big ideas, and themes	Big ideas and themes emerging	Sound conceptual understandings	Conceptual understandings are generalized and applied
Serendipities • Worldview • Student initiative • Technology-laden	Not consciously aware of unexpected results	Unexpected results noted	Unexpected results examined for value	Highly positive unintended outcomes applied and used

Figure A.4   Student Learning—General Rubric

Criteria for Evidence of Student Learning	Not Yet!	On Our Way!	This Is It!	Above and Beyond!
Historical Content	Little evidence of knowledge base	Emerging knowledge of facts and events	Basic understanding of fundamentals	Expert knowledge of critical aspects
Evidence of Research	Slim and questionable list of resources	Variety and number of resources	Sufficient variety and volume of valid references	Robust, annotated listing of classic and current resources
Historical Inferences	No evidence of going beyond the facts	Mostly factual recall level with hints of deeper understanding	Makes appropriate inferences	Makes insightful inferences and applies them to today
Completion of Project	Incomplete and not submitted	Submitted partial project	Submitted complete and sufficient project	Submitted exceptional project with critique

Figure A.5   Curriculum Integration Unit: History Rubric

Criteria for Evidence of Student Learning	Not Yet!	On Our Way!	This Is It!	Above and Beyond!
Content Knowledge	Little evidence of knowledge base	Emerging knowledge of facts and events	Basic understanding of fundamentals	Expert knowledge of critical aspects
Persuasive Essay	Not organized	Organized, yet no strong point of view	Organized, with strong point of view	Well presented and highly convincing
Evidence of Literary References	No evidence of going beyond the facts	Mostly factual recall level with hints of deeper understanding	Makes appropriate inferences	Makes insightful inferences and applies them to today
Application of Skills	Inert knowledge	Understanding evidences with little real application	Applied appropriately	Relevant and robust applications in language arts

Figure A.6   Curriculum Integration Unit: Language Arts Rubric

CONCLUSION

While the assessment of curriculum integration falls into two camps, assessing the actual unit for depth and integrity and assessing student progress, assessment in general is an essential part of the curriculum integration process. And it provides invaluable insight for team discussions and dialogues.

Assessment is the tool that allows teachers to become better at designing rich, robust, and relevant integrated curriculum units of study. It is also what allows teachers to judge the results of implementation of the unit in terms of student learning.

Continue to explore the assessment tool of the scoring rubric. Work with it. Let it evolve over time and enhance the curriculum, instruction, and ongoing assessment of the integrated curriculum process.

References

Agor, S. (2000). *Integrating the ESL standards into classroom practice grades 9–12.* Alexandria, VA: TESOL.

Arredondo, D. E., & Marzano, R. J. (1986). Restructuring schools through the teaching of thinking skills. *Educational Leadership, 43*(8), 28–30.

Barell, J. (1991). *Teaching for thoughtfulness.* New York: Longman.

Beane, J. (1995). *Toward a coherent curriculum.* Alexandria, VA: Association for Supervision and Curriculum Development.

Bellanca, J. (1990). *The cooperative think tank.* Palatine, IL: Skylight Training and Publishing.

Bellanca, J., & Fogarty, R. (1991). *Blueprints for thinking in the cooperative classroom* (2nd ed.). Palatine, IL: SkyLight Training and Publishing.

Beyer, B. (1987). *Practical strategies for the teaching of thinking.* Needham Heights, MA: Allyn & Bacon.

Bloom, A. (1987). *The closing of the American mind.* New York: Simon & Schuster.

Bloom, B. S. (Ed.). (1984). *Taxonomy of educational objectives: The classification of educational goals. Handbook I: Cognitive domain.* New York: Longman.

Brandt, R. (1988). On teaching thinking: A conversation with Arthur Costa. *Educational Leadership, 45*(7), 10–13.

Brown, R. Q. (1991). *Schools of thought: How the politics of literacy shape thinking in the classroom.* San Francisco: Jossey-Bass.

Bruner, J. (1975). *Toward a theory of instruction.* Cambridge, MA: Belknap Press.

Burke, K. (2006). *From standards to rubrics in six steps: Tools for assessing student learning, K–8.* Thousand Oaks, CA: Corwin.

Caine, R. N., & Caine, G. (1990). Understanding a brain-based approach to learning and teaching. *Educational Leadership, 47*(2), 66–70.

Caine, R. N., & Caine, G. (1991). *Making connections: Teaching and the human brain.* Alexandria, VA: Association for Supervision and Curriculum Development.

Caine, R. N., & Caine, G. (1994). *Making connections: Teaching and the human brain* (rev. ed.). Reading, MA: Addison-Wesley.

Caine, R. N., & Caine, G. (1997a). *Education on the edge of possibility.* Alexandria, VA: Association for Supervision and Curriculum Development.

Caine, R. N., & Caine, G. (1997b). *Unleashing the power of perceptual change: The potential of brain-based teaching.* Alexandria, VA: Association for Supervision and Curriculum Development.

Caine, R. N., Caine, G., McClintic, C., & Klimek, K. (2008). *12 brain/mind learning principles in action: Developing executive functions of the human brain* (2nd ed.). Thousand Oaks, CA: Corwin.

Campbell, L., & Campbell, B. (1999). *Multiple intelligences and student achievement: Success stories from six schools.* Alexandria, VA: Association for Supervision and Curriculum Development.

Carbol, B. (1990). *The intermediate program: Learning in British Columbia.* Victoria, British Columbia, Canada: Ministry of Education, Educational Programs.

Carr, J. F., & Harris, D. (2001). *Succeeding with standards: Linking curriculum, assessment, and action planning.* Alexandria, VA: Association for Supervision and Curriculum Development.

Costa, A. L. (1991a). Orchestrating the second wave. *Cogitare, 5*(2), 11–14.

Costa, A. L. (1991b). *The school as a home for the mind.* Palatine, IL: SkyLight Training and Publishing.

Costa, A. L. (1991c). What human beings do when they behave intelligently and how they can become more so. In *Developing minds: A resource book for teaching thinking* (Vol. I, pp. 212–263). Alexandria, VA: Association for Supervision and Curriculum Development.

Costa, A. L., & Garmstom, R. (1988, March). *The art of cognitive coaching: Supervision for intelligent teaching.* Paper presented at the Annual Conference of the Association for Supervision and Curriculum Development, Chicago.

Costa, A., & Kallick, B. (2000a). *Activating and engaging habits of mind.* Alexandria, VA: Association for Supervision and Curriculum Development.

Costa, A., & Kallick, B. (2000b). *Assessing and reporting on habits of mind.* Alexandria, VA: Association for Supervision and Curriculum Development.

Costa, A., & Kallick, B. (2000c). *Discovering and exploring habits of mind.* Alexandria, VA: Association for Supervision and Curriculum Development.

Costa, A., & Kallick, B. (2000d). *Integrating and sustaining habits of mind.* Alexandria, VA: Association for Supervision and Curriculum Development.

De Bono, E. (1985). *Six thinking hats.* Boston: Little, Brown.

Doll, W. (1993). Curriculum possibilities in a "post-future." *Journal of Curriculum and Supervision, 8,* 270–292.

Drake, S. (1998). *Creating integrated curriculum: Proven ways to increase student learning.* Thousand Oaks, CA: Corwin.

Drake, S. (2007). *Creating standards-based integrated curriculum: Aligning curriculum, content, assessment, and instruction* (2nd ed.). Thousand Oaks, CA: Corwin.

Drake, S., & Burns, R. (2004). *Meeting standards through integrated curriculum.* Alexandria, VA: Association for Supervision and Curriculum Development.

Eisner, E. (1991). What really counts in schools. *Educational Leadership, 48*(5), 10–11, 14–17.

Eisner, E. (1994). *Cognition and curriculum reconsidered* (2nd ed.). New York: Teachers College Press.

Elvin, L. (1977). *The place of common sense in educational thought.* London: Unwin Educational Books.

Emerson, R. W. (1982). *Selected essays.* New York: Penguin.

Etim, J. (2005). *Curriculum integration K–12: Theory and practice.* Lanham, MD: University Press of America.

Feuerstein, R. (1980). *Instrumental enrichment.* Baltimore: University Park Press.

Fogarty, R. (1989). *From training to transfer: The role of creativity in the adult learner.* Unpublished doctoral dissertation, Loyola University of Chicago.

Fogarty, R. (1990). *Designs for cooperative interactions.* Palatine, IL: SkyLight Training and Publishing.

Fogarty, R. (1991). Ten ways to integrate curriculum. *Educational Leadership, 49*(2), 61–65.

Fogarty, R. (1993). *How to integrate the curricula: Training manual.* Palatine, IL: IRI/SkyLight Training and Publishing.

Fogarty, R. (1999). *Balanced assessment.* Thousand Oaks, CA: Corwin.

Fogarty, R. (2001a). *Differentiated learning: Different strokes for different folks.* Chicago: Fogarty & Associates.

Fogarty, R. (2001b). *Student learning standards: A blessing in disguise.* Chicago: Fogarty & Associates.

Fogarty, R. (2001c). *Teachers make the difference: A framework for quality.* Chicago: Fogarty & Associates.

Fogarty, R. (2002). *Brain-compatible classrooms.* Arlington Heights, IL: SkyLight Training and Publishing.

Fogarty, R., & Bellanca, J. (1986). *Teach them thinking.* Palatine, IL: SkyLight Training and Publishing.

Fogarty, R., & Bellanca, J. (1989). *Patterns for thinking, patterns for transfer.* Palatine, IL: SkyLight Training and Publishing.

Fogarty, R., & Pete, B. (2007). *How to differentiate learning.* Thousand Oaks, CA: Corwin.

Fogarty, R., & Stoehr, J. (1996). *Integrating curricula with multiple intelligences training manual.* Arlington Heights, IL: IRI/SkyLight Training and Publishing.

Fullan, M. (1991). *The new meaning of educational change.* New York: Teachers College Press.

Gardner, H. (1983). *Frames of mind: The theory of multiple intelligences.* New York: Basic Books.

Gardner, H. (1999). *Intelligence reframed: Multiple intelligences for the 21st century.* New York: Basic Books.

Glass, K. (2007). *Curriculum mapping: A step-by-step guide for creating curriculum year overviews.* Thousand Oaks, CA: Corwin.

Glatthorn, A. (1994). *Developing a quality curriculum.* Alexandria, VA: Association for Supervision and Curriculum Development.

Goleman, D. (1995). *Emotional intelligence: Why it can matter more than IQ.* New York: Bantam Books.

Hale, J. (2007). *A guide to curriculum mapping: Planning, implementing, and sustaining the process.* Thousand Oaks, CA: Corwin.

Hart, L. (1983). *Human brain, human learning.* Kent, WA: Books for Educators.

Hirsch, E. D., Jr. (1987). *Cultural literacy.* Boston: Houghton-Mifflin.

Hirst, P. H. (1964). *Knowledge and curriculum.* London: Routledge.

Hirst, P. H., & Peters, R. S. (1974). The curriculum. In E. Eisner & E. Vallance (Eds.), *Conflicting conceptions of curriculum* (pp. 176–191). Berkeley, CA: McCutchen.

Hord, S., & Loucks, S. (1980). *A concerns-based model for delivery of inservice.* Austin: University of Texas at Austin, Research and Development Center for Teacher Education, CBAM Project.

Howard, D. L. (1994). *Interacting with information: Constructing personal knowledge using written text.* Unpublished doctoral dissertation, University of Hawaii at Manoa.

Hunter, M. (1971). *Teach for transfer.* El Segundo, CA: TIP.

Hyde, A., & Bizar, M. (1989). *Thinking in context.* New York: Longman.

Hyerle, D. (1996). *Visual tools for constructing knowledge.* Alexandria, VA: Association for Supervision and Curriculum Development.

Irujo, S. (2000). *Integrating the ESL standards into classroom practice: Grades 6–8.* Alexandria, VA: TESOL.

Jacobs, H. H. (Ed.). (1989). *Interdisciplinary curriculum: Design and implementation.* Alexandria, VA: Association for Supervision and Curriculum Development.

Jacobs, H. H. (1997). *Mapping the big picture: Integrating curriculum and assessment K–12.* Alexandria, VA: Association for Supervision and Curriculum Development.

Jacobs, H. H. (2004). *Getting results with curriculum mapping.* Alexandria, VA: Association for Supervision and Curriculum Development.

Jacobs, H. H., & Borland, J. H. (1986). The interdisciplinary concept model: Theory and practice. *Gifted Child Quarterly, 30,* 159–163.

Jensen, E. (1999). *Teaching with the brain in mind.* Alexandria, VA: Association for Supervision and Curriculum Development.

Jones, B. F., Palincsar, A., Ogle, D. S., & Carr, E. G. (1987). *Strategic teaching and learning: Cognitive instruction in the content areas.* Alexandria, VA: Association for Supervision and Curriculum Development.

Jones, B. F., Tinzmann, M., Friedman, L., & Walker, B. (1987). *Teaching thinking skills: English/language arts.* Washington, DC: National Educational Association.

Joyce, B. R. (1986). *Improving America's schools.* New York: Longman.

Joyce, B. R., & Showers, B. (1980). Improving inservice training: The message of research. *Educational Leadership, 37,* 379–382, 384–385.

Joyce, B. R., & Showers, B. (1983). *Power and staff development through research and training.* Alexandria, VA: Association for Supervision and Curriculum Development.

Kallick, B., & Colosimo, J. (2008). *Using curriculum mapping and assessment data to improve learning.* Thousand Oaks, CA: Corwin.

Kentucky Educational Television. (1993). *Integrated learning video series* [Videocassettes]. Lexington, KY: Author.

King, K. (2006). *Integrating the National Science Education Standards into classroom practice.* Upper Saddle River, NJ: Prentice Hall.

Kirkland, L., Aldridge, J., & Kuby, P. (2006). *Integrating environmental print across the curriculum, PreK–3: Making literacy instruction meaningful.* Thousand Oaks, CA: Corwin.

Kovalic, S. (1993). *ITI: The model: Integrated thematic instruction.* Oak Creek, AZ: Books for Educators.

Lawton, D. (1975). *Class, culture and curriculum.* Boston: Routledge.

Lazear, D. (1999). *Eight ways of knowing* (3rd ed.). Arlington Heights, IL: SkyLight Training and Publishing.

Marcus, S. (2007). *The hungry brain: The nutrition cognition connection.* Thousand Oaks, CA: Corwin.

Marcus, S. (n.d.). *Are four food groups enough?* Unpublished doctoral dissertation, Walden University, Minneapolis, MN.

Martin, H. (1996). *Integrating mathematics across the curriculum.* Arlington Heights, IL: SkyLight Training and Publishing.

Marzano, R. J. (2004). *Building background knowledge for academic achievement: Research on what works in schools.* Alexandria, VA: Association for Supervision and Curriculum Development.

Marzano, R. J., Pickering, D., & Brandt, R. (1990). Integrating instruction programs through dimensions of learning. *Educational Leadership, 47*(5), 17–24.

Marzano, R. J., Pickering, D., & Pollock, J. (2001). *Classroom instruction that works: Research-based strategies for increasing student achievement.* Alexandria, VA: Association for Supervision and Curriculum Development.

Maute, J. (1989). Cross-curricular connections. *Middle School Journal, 20*(4), 20–22.

Meeth, L. R. (1978). Interdisciplinary studies: Integration of knowledge and experience. *Change, 10,* 6–9.

Meinbach, A., Fredericks, A., & Rothlein, L. (2000). *The complete guide to thematic units: Creating the integrated curriculum.* Norwood, MA: Christopher-Gordan.

Ministry of Education. (1991). *Integration: A framework for discussion* (Draft 2). Victoria, British Columbia, Canada: Author.

Missouri Department of Elementary and Secondary Education. (1996). *Standards of learning.* Jefferson City, MO: Author.

Osborn, A. F. (1963). *Applied imagination.* New York: Scribner.

Parnes, S. J. (1975). *Aha! Insights into creative behavior.* Buffalo, NY: D.O.K.

Perkins, D. N. (1986). *Knowledge as design.* Hillsdale, NJ: Lawrence Erlbaum.

Perkins, D. N. (1988, March). *Thinking frames.* Paper presented at the Association for Supervision and Curriculum Development Conference, Approaches to Teaching Thinking, Alexandria, VA.

Perkins, D. N. (1989). Selecting fertile themes for integrated learning. In H. H. Jacobs (Ed.), *Interdisciplinary curriculum: Design and implementation* (pp. 67–76). Alexandria, VA: Association for Supervision and Development.

Perkins, D. N., Goodrich, H., Tishman, S., & Owen J. M. (1994). *Thinking connections: Learning to think and thinking to learn.* Reading, MA: Addison-Wesley.

Perkins, D. N., & Salomon, G. (1988). Teaching for transfer. *Educational Leadership, 46*(1), 22–32.

Perkins, D. N., & Salomon, G. (1989). Are cognitive skills content bound? *Educational Researcher, 18*(1), 16–25.

Perna, D. M., & Davis, J. R. (2000). *Aligning standards and curriculum for classroom success.* Arlington Heights, IL: SkyLight Training and Publishing.

Pete, B., & Fogarty, R. (2003a). *Nine best practices that make the difference.* Thousand Oaks, CA: Corwin.

Pete, B., & Fogarty, R. (2003b). *Twelve brain principles that make the difference.* Thousand Oaks, CA: Corwin.

Pete, B., & Fogarty, R. (2005). *Close the achievement gap: Simple strategies that work.* Thousand Oaks, CA: Corwin.

Pete, B., & Sambo, C. (2004). *Data! Dialogue! Decisions! The data difference.* Thousand Oaks, CA: Corwin.

Piaget, J. (1972). *The epistemology of interdisciplinary relationships.* Paris: Organization for Economic Cooperation and Development.

Posner, M. I., & Keele, S. W. (1973). Skill learning. In R. M. W. Travers (Ed.). *Second handbook of research on teaching* (pp. 805–821). Chicago: Rand McNally.

Ravitch, D. (1985). Why educators resist a basic required curriculum. In B. Gross & R. Gross (Eds.), *The great school debate* (pp. 199–203). New York: Simon & Schuster.

Ravitch, D., & Finn, C. (1985). The humanities: A truly challenging course of study. In B. Gross & R. Gross (Eds.), *The great school debate* (pp. 308–329). New York: Simon & Schuster.

Resnick, L. B., & Klopfer, L. (1989). *Toward the thinking curriculum: Current cognitive research. 1989 ASCD Yearbook.* Alexandria, VA: Association for Supervision and Curriculum Development.

Richards, M. C. (1980). *The public school and the education of the whole person.* Philadelphia: Pilgrim Press.

Ronis, D. (2001). *Problem-based learning for math and science: Integrating inquiry and the Internet.* Arlington Heights, IL: SkyLight Training and Publishing.

Samway, K. (2000). *Integrating the ESL standards into classroom practice: Pre-K–2.* Alexandria, VA: TESOL.

Sergiovanni, T. (1987). Will we ever have a true profession? *Educational Leadership, 44*(8), 44–49.

Shoemaker, B. (1989). Integrative education: A curriculum for the twenty-first century. *OSSC Bulletin, 33*(2).

Shoemaker, B. (1991). Education 2000: Integrated curriculum. *Phi Delta Kappan, 72,* 793–797.

Silver, H., Strong, R., & Perini, M. (2000). *So each may learn: Integrating learning styles and multiple intelligences.* Alexandria, VA: Association for Supervision and Curriculum Development.

Smallwood, B. (2000). *Integrating the ESL standards into classroom practice: Grades 3–5.* Alexandria, VA: TESOL.

Sousa, D. (1995). *How the brain learns: A classroom teacher's guide.* Reston, VA: National Association of Secondary Schools.

Sprenger, M. (1999). *Learning and memory: The brain in action.* Alexandria, VA: Association for Supervision and Curriculum Development.

Sternberg, R. J. (1984). How can we teach intelligence? *Educational Leadership, 42*(1), 38–48.

Sternberg, R. J. (1986). *Intelligence applied: Understanding and increasing your intellectual skills.* New York: Harcourt Brace Jovanovich.

Sylwester, R. (1995). *Celebration of neurons: An educator's guide to the human brain.* Alexandria, VA: Association for Supervision and Curriculum Development.

Tomlinson, C. (1999). *The differentiated classroom: Responding to the needs of all learners.* Alexandria, VA: Association for Supervision and Curriculum Development.

Tomlinson, C. (2001). *How to differentiate instruction in mixed-ability classrooms.* Alexandria, VA: Association for Supervision and Curriculum Development.

Tomlinson, C., & Demirski-Allen, S. (2000). *Leadership for differentiating schools and classrooms.* Alexandria, VA: Association for Supervision and Curriculum Development.

Treadwell, M. (2001). *1001 best Internet sites for educators.* Arlington Heights, IL: SkyLight Training and Publishing.

Tyler, R. W. (1949). *Basic principles of curriculum and instruction.* Chicago: University of Chicago Press.

Tyler, R. W. (1986–1987). The five most significant curriculum events in the twentieth century. *Educational Leadership, 44*(4), 36–38.

Vars, G. F. (1987). *Interdisciplinary teaching in the middle grades.* Columbus, OH: National Middle School Association.

Wiggins, G., & McTighe, J. (1998). *Understanding by design.* Alexandria, VA: Association for Supervision and Curriculum Development.

Williams, R. (2002). *Cooperative learning: A standard for high achievement.* Thousand Oaks, CA: Corwin.

Williams, R. (2003). *Higher order thinking: Challenging all students to achieve.* Thousand Oaks, CA: Corwin.

Williams, R. (2006a). *36 tools for building spirit in learning communities.* Thousand Oaks, CA: Corwin.

Williams, R. (2006b). *More than 50 ways to build team consensus* (2nd ed.). Thousand Oaks, CA: Corwin.

Williams, R. (2007). *Multiple intelligences for differentiated learning.* Thousand Oaks, CA: Corwin.

Williams, R. (2008). *Twelve roles of facilitators for school change* (2nd ed.). Thousand Oaks, CA: Corwin.

Wittrock, M. C. (1967). Replacement and nonreplacement strategies in children's problem solving. *Journal of Educational Psychology, 58*(2), 69–74.

Index

CORWIN
A SAGE Company

The Corwin logo—a raven striding across an open book—represents the union of courage and learning. Corwin is committed to improving education for all learners by publishing books and other professional development resources for those serving the field of PreK–12 education. By providing practical, hands-on materials, Corwin continues to carry out the promise of its motto: **"Helping Educators Do Their Work Better."**